THE GENIUS OF PURITANISM

Foreword by

D. MARTYN LLOYD-JONES

THE GENIUS OF PURITANISM

PETER LEWIS

I am the true vine   *John 15 v1*

Soli Deo Gloria Publications
...for instruction in righteousness...

Soli Deo Gloria Publications
P.O. Box 451, Morgan, PA 15064
(412) 221-1901/FAX 221-1902

*

The Genius of Puritanism was first published in 1977
by Carey Publications in England. This Soli Deo
Gloria reprint is 1996. Printed in the USA.
All rights reserved.

*

ISBN 1-57358-031-7

FOREWORD

READILY WRITE THIS WORD OF COM-
mendation for this volume. I well remember
how Mr. Lewis as a student showed a real living
interest in the writings of the Puritans, and how
he came into my vestry at Westminster Chapel
from time to time to tell me of various purchases
he had been fortunate to make, and at times to
lend me some of these.

I am particularly glad that he has clearly kept
up this early interest and has continued his wide reading in, and
study of the Puritans. This volume provides abundant proof of
that.

He has chosen to concentrate attention on the preaching and
pastoral activities of those remarkable men of the 17th century,
while explaining in an introductory chapter that their original and
primary interest was in the nature of the Church.

He thus provides an excellent foretaste of the rich meal that
readers of the works of the Puritans can enjoy.

His arrangement of the matter – the brief biographical touches,
the judicious selections threaded into a continuing theme etc. – is
brilliant.

Here some of the leading Puritans are allowed to speak for
themselves, and I am sure that many who read this book will be
stimulated to acquire and read the works out of which these selections
have been made. Nothing but great spiritual good can result from
that, both in individual lives, and in the life of the churches.

D. M. LLOYD-JONES.

July, 1975

EDICATED TO THE MEMORY of Dr. Ernest F. Kevan, late Principal of the London Bible College; Puritan scholar and theologian.

He made the genius of Puritanism clear in his teaching and visible in his demeanour and so became his students' mentor in life and learning.

PREFACE

PREFACE AFFORDS THE WRITER OPPOR-tunity to be just a little more personal than he could be in the body of a book. Thus I may perhaps confess here, to my three great motives in writing this book in the way I have done. First of all I have tried to recall the paramount importance which right preaching has in the Nonconformist and biblical tradition – and that for both preachers and hearers. Secondly, I have sought to show pastors of our own day the way in which that most biblical race of men outside the Testaments, namely the Puritans, applied a deep doctrinal sense and spiritual wisdom to the various problems, especially depressions and discouragements, under which God's people have always had to labour in this life. Thirdly, I have sought to stimulate the reader not merely to be content with reading secondary works about the Puritans but to *read the Puritan writings* (now so frequently reprinted) themselves. That explains why I have sought at almost every point to let the Puritans speak for themselves: and as an author will often be forgiven anything but dullness, I have sought to avoid that most reprehensible of literary sins by choosing quotations and extracts which exhibit the winsome and colloquial style of the Puritan divines. In all this it has been my hope that many will be led to a wiser and deeper exploration into those works which have been for too long 'treasures of darkness'.

To the patience and kind assistance of the publishers and their keen-eyed proof-readers; to the long-standing encouragement and kindness of Dr. D. M. Lloyd-Jones whose patronage itself deserves an 'epistle dedicatory' and to my wife Valerie who has so well played her 'Margaret' to my 'Baxter', I remain under an obligation which I here acknowledge but can scarce repay.

HYSON GREEN BAPTIST CHURCH
NOTTINGHAM

CONTENTS

INTRODUCTION

THE CHARACTER AND COURSE OF ENGLISH PURITANISM

T IS QUESTIONABLE WHETHER CHRIStians can ever look for the regeneration of the world before they seek the reformation of the Church. If we are horrified at the state of the world in our generation, can we be less anxious about the state of the Church within that world? If the light that is in the world be darkness, how great is that darkness! And in a day when, in the very Church of God, we too often see law denigrated, grace abused, truth neglected as 'mere doctrine', and experience placed on a par with revelation, we have urgent need to ask (without fault) why 'the former times were better than these'.

To neglect God's work in the past is to neglect his Word in the present, for throughout history God has raised up men and movements whose great work was to expound and apply that Word to their own generation, and by implication to ours also. Such men were the Puritans and such a movement was Puritanism.

The definitions of 'Puritan' and 'Puritanism' have been, since their earliest use in England, a matter of crowded debate and widespread confusion. National, political and social elements which were closely allied with the idea of Puritanism at various stages of its progress have largely obscured the vital religious and spiritual meaning of the term. Without attempting an exhaustive definition we may say that essential Puritanism grew out of three great areas: the New Testament pattern of personal piety, sound doctrine and a properly ordered Church-life, and it is the mingling and blending together of all three of these emphases which made English Puritanism the astonishment and the inspiration it was and is still. As it is largely out of an examination of these three areas that an understanding of Puritanism will come, we shall turn to each of them in succession before giving a brief account of the history of the movement.

William Ames, a great leader in the movement, once defined 'divinity' as 'the doctrine of living to God' and in making the definition he epigrammatically described the whole moving spirit of Puritanism. For Puritanism was not merely a set of rules or a larger creed, but a life-force: a vision and a compulsion which saw the beauty of a holy life and moved towards it, marvelling at the possibilities and thrilling to the satisfaction of a God-centred life. Moreover, iron discipline was combined with fervent devotion, saving the Puritan from a fitful mysticism on the one hand and a mere worldly religion on the other – and it was this marvellous marriage of law and grace which was not the least notable feature of Puritan piety. Every area of life came under the influence of God and the guidance of the Word. Each day began and ended with searching, unhurried and devout personal and family prayer. Each task, whether professional or manual, was done to the glory of God and with a scrupulous eye to his perfect will. Every relationship, business or personal, was regulated by spiritual principles. Hours free from labour were gladly and zealously employed in the study of the Scriptures, attendance upon public worship, 'godly converse' or intense witness and every other means which contributed to the soul's good. In a word, the 'great business of godliness' dominated the ardent believer's ambitions and called forth all his energies. We may say that to a large extent Puritanism succeeded where other more cloistered ideologies failed, because here men *embodied* true doctrine so that Puritanism was made visible before men. Men *saw* on earth lives that were not earthly, lives that touched their own at so many points, yet which rolled on into a moral and spiritual continent of breathtaking landscape. Indeed, it is not too much to say that Puritans *were* Puritanism proper – for Puritanism was sainthood visible.

With vitality of spiritual life, there was, of necessity, a doctrinal rectitude and firmness that based the biblical life upon biblical thought. Richard Baxter wrote at the beginning of one of his books: 'Sound doctrine makes a sound judgment, a sound heart, a sound conversation [life] and a sound conscience' – and if it was otherwise, then either the doctrine was not sound or it was not soundly understood! Piety does not grow out of the ground nor does it materialise out of the air. True godliness is born, not of mystical experience, nor of educated nature, but of the royal marriage of Truth with Grace, and the godly Puritan was a child of both parents. The literature of Puritanism is full of folios on Christian doctrine, leaving the mind with the impression of something majestic and it is beyond controversy that the men who wrote them were ennobled by the very doctrine they expounded. Their minds were as massive as their folios and their piety was not dwarfed by either. Vastly Calvinistic in their theological tradition, they treasured a high conception of the sovereignty of God in providence and grace, and reflected this in the tranquillity with which they were able to carry themselves in the stormiest experiences and the forcefulness with which they were able to show the desperate needs and the unfailing resort of fallen man. If their doctrine of God elevated them, their doctrine of sin humbled them. Recognising their own propensity to sin as well as the potential for evil in fallen human nature at large they did not tire of exposing sin as the plague of plagues and root of all man's ills. In their books and sermons they followed the devious course of sin in all its guises, demolishing self-confidence and pointing men to that salvation which could be of grace alone.

A third major characteristic of Puritanism was the place it gave to the doctrine of the Church. Indeed, Puritanism as a movement largely began as an endeavour to reform the face of the English Church, and to do so according to the Scriptures and the Scriptures alone. Neither the civil nor ecclesiastical powers, they maintained, had the authority to add to, subtract from, or modify the sufficient, definitive teaching of the New Testament in its pattern of Church government and Church life. It was for this reason that they rejected Anglican ceremonies and vestments, and Episcopal church government which, being the outgrowth of tradition rather than the New Testament, continued to make the Anglican Church less than consistent with some of the basic principles of the Reformation. When either monarch or bishops attempted to enforce tradition or hinder reformation, then what was at stake was not the wearing or not wearing of a few official costumes in public worship, nor the expedient government of the Church by this or that method of organisation; but rather the whole regulating principle of the Church of Christ on earth. The vital questions which so dominated Puritan thought lay here. In matters spiritual and ecclesiastical, was the Church to order her own course as distinct from the monarch, and were the Scriptures to order the Church as distinct from ecclesiastical tradition or expedience? In a word, who rules the Church and the spiritual realm of life – God or man? These were fundamental questions. Had they not been on countless lips in the days of Luther and Calvin? The answer of the Puritans was a confident affirmative for the freedom of the Church under the sole sovereignty of the Scriptures. For this they were prepared to suffer with a determination as grim as it was serene.

Having seen some of the basic characteristics of Puritanism, we turn to a brief outline of the history of the movement. Although its origins are to be found earlier, the Puritan movement may be said to have begun around 1559 with the Act of Uniformity and to have ended as such during the second half of the seventeenth century – perhaps officially with the Act of Uniformity of 1662 and the ensuing 'Great Ejection'. Thus it began under Elizabeth I who suspected it, grew under James I who feared it, increased in power under Charles I and his Archbishop, William Laud, who despised it, gained a brief but august ascendency under Cromwell who honoured it, and ended under Charles II and his bishops who hated it.

Ecclesiastically, the Puritans were convinced, as we have seen, that the Reformation in England had, because of political expediency, been stunted before it had properly conformed the Church to the simplicity of the New Testament model. In the sixteenth century the first generation of Puritans tried to bring about the necessary reforms in church polity and worship largely by political means. Elizabeth had produced a 'settlement' which trod a middle way between Roman Catholicism on the one hand and Genevan Calvinism on the other. This was the archetype of the Anglican Church of our own day. While rejecting many of the political and religious tenets of Catholicism, Elizabeth, with the determination to retain full control of Church as well as State and to unite as far as possible the various elements within her realm, dismissed the 'extremism' of the Puritan faction within 'her' Church, and sought to impose conformity to her Anglican model by the Acts of Supremacy and Uniformity of 1559 and the fateful Convocation of 1563.

The Puritans were no match for Elizabeth in the field of politics and from this time the movement, politically defeated, began to channel its considerable energies in other directions. Having failed to reform the Church from the top down, by parliamentary legislation, the Puritans sought with greater vigour than ever to do so from the bottom up by the persuasion of pulpit, press and personal influence. From here on the real story of Puritanism is the story of its spiritual growth and power, and the history of the progress of Puritanism becomes not the record of councils and convocations, of legislation and counter-legislation, but the history of men whose crusade for a godly Church and a godly State could not be either much hindered or much helped by parliaments and their acts. Puritanism became a grass-roots movement which the legislative scythe could limit but not destroy.

Yet, although Puritanism as a movement grew up within the framework of the Anglican Church, it is questionable whether we can ever regard it as an outgrowth of Anglicanism, much less a development of it or a form of it. When one sees the early radical differences between the Puritan mind and the Anglican mentality – as shown for instance in the differences between John Knox and Richard Cox at the English Church at Frankfurt, and between Hooper and Cranmer in the vestiarian controversy in England – one begins to ask if Puritanism was not always a cuckoo in the Anglican nest, in it but not really of it – and that from the beginning! True, under the exigencies of the times, the two for long lay close together like two sticks lying in such close proximity that they seem at first to be one, but with the advance of the years and the increasing intractability of the politically and episcopally-controlled Anglican Church, Puritanism irresistibly showed itself to be a species which had a life of its own, having a separate identity and being capable of a separate development. This resulted in and was demonstrated, by first, the successive ventures of independency in the non-conformity of individuals; later, by the course of the early Separatists; later still in the course of the Pilgrim Fathers during the reign of James I, and finally in the massive exodus of 'The Two Thousand' at the Ejectment of 1662.

During this course, Puritanism must not be thought of as 'tailing off' into a separatist Nonconformity, for its story is one of amazing growth, advance and development into that full-blown Nonconformity which alone could express Puritanism's true nature. The movement spread, from the last days of Elizabeth I, by the emergence of hundreds of men dedicated in their young ministries to a common vision and a common spirit which bound them together as no mere party machine could ever do. This vision did not fade with the years, but rather its lineaments became increasingly clear, and, to the army of new reformers, increasingly thrilling under the influence of the leaders of the movement. The volumes of William Perkins loaded the shelves of many who never heard his forceful preaching at Cambridge, and the famous *Seven Treatises* of Richard Rogers of Wethersfield in Essex fanned a thousand sparks into a thousand flames with their archetypal standards of Puritan piety. In the reigns of James I and Charles I the popular works of Richard Sibbes watered a soil well seeded by a former generation,

and throughout the succeeding period of Puritan prominence in the
time of Cromwell's power, the ready pens of Owen, Baxter, Goodwin,
and a score of others united those whom distance kept apart.

During these long years the Puritans had troubles-a-plenty and
needed every encouragement and inspiration. James I (1603-1625)
countered his Presbyterian cradle with an episcopalian cross and,
seeing that Puritanism meant a serious limiting of his kingly 'rights'
and powers, swore to the Puritan leaders that he would 'harrie them
out of the land'. But while James 'harried' them out of Old
England, God hurried them into the New, and others who did not
go to the Americas sheltered in Dutch ports until better days should
come. The majority stayed at home to weather the storm which,
when James' crown sat on the head of his son Charles I (1625-1649),
grew in force. But so also did the ominous cross-winds that countered it, for Puritanism did not stand alone in these turbulent years.
The Puritan mind gave rise to thoughts on spiritual principles which
were to have far-reaching effects in secular as well as religious life –
in the State as well as the Church. Puritanism emphasised that the
individual could never be regarded as a mere pawn of the times.
Did he not have an immortal soul? Had not the Son of God himself
come to die for such, as much as for princes and prelates? Also,
the Puritan doctrine of the place of conscience, its laws and liberties
in the life of the individual, placed the subject over against his
monarch and not under his feet, and from his new position Everyman
gained a new and very different perspective. This was no mere
change in abstract thought: it was to change the face of English
history. The erosion of English liberties by Charles I and the
attempts by his bigoted High-Church Archbishop, William Laud,
to manacle the free-souled Protestantism of so great a part of the
nation, drew down upon the heads of that regime the wrath of both
an outraged piety and a newly-awakened sense of the dignity and
responsibilities of the individual. Out of this emerged a newly
militant 'political Puritanism' which was to lead through Parliamen-
tarianism to, in many cases, a full-blown Republicanism. It was
this revolution which gave religious Puritanism, at last, its halcyon
period of real liberty and when the Civil Wars (1642-1648) had
drawn the teeth of Royalism and Prelacy alike, Puritanism, under
the enlightened and prestigious rule of Oliver Cromwell (1654-
1658), enjoyed its fullest expression and greatest expansion.

However, political and religious Puritanism were to prove un-
comfortable bed-fellows. Many Puritans were still moderate
Royalists, many had little love for, and much distrust of Cromwell,

GVILIELMVS PERKINSVS STHEO D.
PERNSVS Cristi defendens dogmatatalis
Vultu erat, ingenium scripta facunda probant

William Perkins stood at the fountain head of Puritanism's new and vigorous development in the last decades of the sixteenth century. Perkins' great ministry at Cambridge resulted in his becoming mentor of an army of young men who developed his expository and pastoral emphases.

CANTAB: · EFFIGIES · DOCTIS: VIRI · RICHARDI ROGERS · THEOLOGVS

*The Pourtraicture of the most tremly reuerend
faithfull Painefull and Profitable Minister of Gods
word M͏ʳ Richard Rogers Preacher of the word
of God at Wethersfeild in Essex.*

*Richard Rogers of Wethersfield in Essex—a great father-figure
in the Puritan movement. His famous 'Seven Treatises' on the
godly life provided the pattern of Puritan piety for many years.
On once being told by 'a gentleman', 'Mr. Rogers, I like you
and your company very well, only you are too precise.' 'Oh
sir,' replied Rogers, 'I serve a precise God.' There spoke
Puritanism!*

and of the Puritan clergy few could be found who had minds as broad, and political senses as acute as the Protector. 'The rule of the Saints,' throughout its various phases had within itself the seeds of its own destruction. There were many, for instance, in the dominant Presbyterian party who could be as narrow and harsh as their erstwhile Episcopal persecutors, while more moderate Puritans, such as were of the short-lived Barebones Parliament, were hopelessly fragmented, and it shortly became clear that if the Puritan minister could be incomparable in the pulpit, the Puritan politician could be insufferable in Parliament. The political groupings of Puritans, and of Republicans generally, fragmented both the rulers and the ruled. One hand alone was strong enough to hold so unruly a helm, and when the hand of 'Oliver Protector' was stilled in death, the ship of State was quickly guided from the real – or supposed – rocks of anarchy into the still – and stagnant – waters of a new period of monarchy.

The swift resumption of the English throne by the Stuart line, in Charles II, after the death of Cromwell and the downfall of his Republic, might have seemed the end of the 'Puritan revolution', and so it would have been if Puritanism had been merely a political revolution of the Civil Wars. However, we have seen enough to show that behind this, and rising above it at many points, was a larger and purely spiritual Puritan revolution: one that began long before Oliver's hand closed around an English sword – and one that would survive when that sword was laid down. However, after 1660, a Royalist Parliament, spiced once again with High-Church bishops, recommenced in earnest the persecution of the Puritans – a persecution which refused to distinguish between political and spiritual Puritanism. Soon the Prayer Book was re-imposed, having been so altered for its renewed imposition that there was justification in many eyes for one Puritan minister's summary criticism of it as 'defective in necessaries, redundant in superfluities, dangerous in some things, disputable in many, disorderly in all'! This imposition was swiftly followed by the notorious Act of Uniformity (1662) to which, as well its architects knew, there was no chance of the Puritans as a whole submitting. This Act, as well as demanding 'unfeigned assent and consent' to everything in the new edition of the Prayer Book, required, among other things, the renunciation of Presbyterian ordination and a submission to Episcopal re-ordination. It required also an oath of allegiance to Charles which included an abjuration of the 'Solemn League and Covenant' of 1643 which had justified the resistance of Parliament to

Charles I. It was no surprise that many Puritans considered the renunciation of their previous ordinations as blasphemous and, for all their willingness to be loyal under the new king, the formal abjuration of the once-sworn Covenant as perjury; nor was it less than expected that the vast majority of Puritans found the demand for sworn assent and consent to the varied contents of the new Prayer Book a similar outrage upon true piety.

The inevitable followed and, before the winter of 1662, almost two thousand of the Church's best men had been expelled from their ministries – cast out into the world, many destitute, with their families. There followed a series of cruel and ingenious Acts aimed at preventing the ejected from preaching, even privately, under penalties varying from the petty to the vicious. Thereafter also, a campaign of libel and slander ensued in an endeavour to sully and besmirch the whole Puritan movement as one composed of sectaries, fanatics and rebels, ignorant and unbalanced men. It was soon forgotten that almost all of them were the scholarly products of Oxford and Cambridge Universities, many of them men of culture and much moderation and all men of irreproachable piety.

The question remains – did all this achieve the destruction and failure of Puritanism? The answer of history stands: no, it did not. Puritanism, not destroyed but metamorphosed by persecution and political defeat, passed over into a thorough-going religious Nonconformity, and, as such, began a new stage in its own and in the nation's religious development: a stage which survived the long period of Stuart persecution and saw the restoration of old liberties in the Glorious Revolution of 1688; a stage which survived, too, the more insidious, but no less dangerous period of widespread apathy and hardening in the earlier decades of the eighteenth century; a stage which survived to begin the notable period of missionary expansion that stretched from the Baptist, William Carey, in the 1790s, to the massive missionary movements of Nonconformity in the Victorian era, a stage which survives in our own day in evangelical Nonconformity for which the lives and writings of the Puritan brotherhood stand as an abiding monument and an unquenched inspiration.

I

THE PURITAN IN THE PULPIT

A study in the Puritan doctrine of preaching

THE PURITAN PREACHERS

E HAVE POINTED OUT ALREADY THAT the real and larger Puritan revolution was bloodless, spiritual and verbal. In this greater conflict the Puritan pulpit proved to be the place of mightiest assault on world, flesh and devil. From the despised 'prophesyings' of Elizabeth's lay to the hounded conventicles of Restoration England the Puritan preaching was a power in the land. It was by turns tolerated, encouraged and opposed; it was applauded, 'refuted' and mocked; it was venerated and it was blasphemed – but it could not be, and never was, ignored!

Its much-minimised and now almost forgotten popularity among the people is not difficult to explain for the Puritan preachers, more than any others, made true religion the *possession* of their people. They did not show them the 'Promised Land' from afar but led them into it, pressed upon them its fruits and bade them boldly claim all its territories. Their congregations 'possessed' the sermons: the colloquial style of these was winsome, abounding in similes and metaphors from every-day life and alive with anecdote and illustration, thus bringing home to the meanest capacity truths precious to the humblest soul. The Bible likewise was urged upon them as their rightful possession and was thoroughly 'opened' to the people and shown to provide an abundant sufficiency of divine direction and unfailing comfort for immortal souls in all-too-mortal situations. Finally, the whole power of godliness was pressed upon their flocks as theirs to appropriate and exercise in the life of faith. Under such ministries the Puritan congregations felt that they were 'kings and priests unto God' indeed – and strove to live as such!

In order to achieve all this, the Puritans brought into their preaching both the learning of the study and the practicability of the market-place. Their sermons savoured of close meditation in the closet and no less close observation in the street. Their preaching was lively because it dealt with life as it was. If their bodies were confined to narrow limits in those parochial days, their prayers roamed country and metropolis, and the sermons born of those prayers hummed with the activity of a restless age. If they were heavenly-minded, the Puritan preachers were no less down-to-earth. No doubt the 'noble negligence' of Richard Baxter's style, for example, and the polish-free earnestness of his pulpit appeals were due in no small part to the years spent as a Roundhead chaplain, smelling the gunpowder of immediate reality whilst thinking out the abstractions of metaphysics.

The Puritan preachers, however much their hearers donned 'Sunday best' for church, seemed always to see them in the shop-apron or the farm-gear of the work-a-day world and aimed, not only to arrest their attention on the Lord's day, but to affect their lives and hearts in the stores and fields during the days that followed. Like Baxter, they preached for eternity as well as time, to the heart as well as to the mind and, like him in his celebrated couplet, they all 'preached as never sure to preach again', each 'as a dying man to dying men'. It was thus that the Puritan of the sixteenth and seventeenth centuries caught the ear, stirred the emotions and directed the lives of his contemporaries high and low, learned and illiterate, educating in spiritual truth and elevating in spiritual power the people committed to his charge. And it was thus that by the even quality of its matter, by the forceful sincerity and spiritual power of its utterance, by the soundness of its doctrine and the thoroughness of its practical application the Puritan pulpit produced the golden age of evangelical preaching in England.

Let us now look more closely, though briefly, at some of the Puritan preachers who are mentioned in the following pages.

William Perkins (1558-1602)

William Perkins was a patriarchal figure in English Puritanism and his preaching in Cambridge proved to be a formative influence upon the Puritan movement in its seventeenth-century development. An accomplished theologian (he was a fellow of Christ's College and Lecturer at St. Andrews) his preaching remained clear, practical and very powerful. While full enough of 'the terrors of law and of God', one of its most significant features was its dealing with troubled consciences and here, in the realm of casuistry, Perkins largely stimulated in England a most notable feature of Puritanism and one which had, to a great extent, been the prerogative (often much-abused) of the Roman Catholic Church. Later Puritan writers who were eminent in dealing with the doubts and fears of the troubled soul, writers such as William Ames, were first guided towards this ministry by Perkins' lectures upon the subject. By this, as by his thorough and typically Puritan standards of expository preaching and strict and pious living, the younger generation of Puritans was immeasurably influenced by 'Perkins our wonder' (Fletcher).

Henry Smith (1560-1591)

Henry Smith was, in his brief day, the orator *par excellence* of the movement. Less developed than later Puritan sermons, Smith's had 'the root of the matter' in them and were clothed in a rich, native style of eloquence. Crowds flocked to hear 'silver-tongued Smith' as he was called, at St. Clement Danes, London where he was lecturer, and loved to sit utterly under his spell. Writes that quaintest of old historians, Thomas Fuller: 'His church was so crowded with auditors that persons of good quality brought their own pews with them, I mean their legs, to stand thereupon in the alleys (aisles). Their ears did so attend to his lips, their hearts to their ears, that he held the rudder of their affections in his hands so that he could steer them whither he was pleased – and he was pleased to steer them only to God's glory and their own good.'

Dying at thirty-one we may well say 'he lived long in a little time'. It seems incredible that Henry Smith's London ministry lasted only three years but during this period he took the city by storm, was suspended for his Puritanism and was so popular that printers' men took down his sermons as he preached and rushed them immediately into print willy-nilly. His printed sermons continued to be, for generations, a household book and passed through a very large number of editions.

Thomas Taylor (1576-1633)

Thomas Taylor's name became illustrious in the generation following Perkins and Smith. First a despiser of the Puritan cause and then a sufferer for it, his Nonconformity drove him from a lectureship in Hebrew at Christ's College, Cambridge to the 'open ministry' and he laboured at Watford, Reading and London. His years at Reading marked a period when he inspired many young Puritans into the ministry and the last seven years of his life at London were full of honour and prestige. From his ever-busy pen flowed a host of works whose concentrated wealth of matter and imaginative style (even his prefaces read like exciting sermons) show why he was styled among his contemporaries 'the illuminated doctor'.

John Rogers (d. 1636)

John Rogers, of Dedham in Essex, laboured with famed success as one of the most forceful and 'awakening' preachers of his age. His complete self-forgetfulness in the pulpit led him into occasional extremes of turbulent, tempestuous and even desperate delivery (his packed congregations never forgot the occasion when he imitated the screams of the souls in hell!), but the solid substance of his matter and the transparent earnestness of his manner rescued his preaching from the merely eccentric, and provoked from the contemporary Bishop Brownrigg the admission, 'John Rogers will do more good with his wild notes than we with our set music'. Another contemporary, a Puritan, Richard Steele, recalls that it was a saying among the godly at that time, 'Let us go to Dedham to fetch fire'. John Rogers, though a rugged preacher, was a great soul-winner and reduced many, including, on one unforgettable occasion, the great Thomas Goodwin (then a young man) to helpless tears of repentance and gratitude toward God.

The occasion of this last reference provides us with a memorable account of high drama in the Puritan pulpit. Goodwin himself told the story to the renowned John Howe years later. Howe recalls the incident: 'Mr. Rogers was . . . on the subject of the Scriptures. And in that sermon he falls into an expostulation with the people about their neglect of the Bible. . . . He personates God to the people telling them, "Well, I have trusted you so long with my Bible: you have slighted it; it lies in such and such a house all covered with dust and cobwebs. You care not to look at it. Do you use my Bible so? Well you shall have my Bible no longer". And he takes up the Bible from his cushion and seemed as if he were going away with it and carrying it from them; but immediately [he] turns again and personates the people to God, falls down on

his knees, cries and pleads most earnestly, "Lord, whatsoever thou
dost to us take not thy Bible from us; kill our children, burn our
houses, destroy our goods; only spare us thy Bible, only take not
away thy Bible". And then he personates God again to the people,
"Say you so? Well, I will try you a little while longer; and here is
my Bible for you, I will see how you use it, whether you will love it
more, whether you will value it more, whether you will observe it
more, whether you will practise it more and live more according to
it".' Howe continues to recall the effect of all this: 'By these actions
(as the Doctor told me) he put all the congregation into so strange
a posture that he never saw any congregation in his life; the place
was a mere Bochim the people generally (as it were) deluged with
their own tears; and he told me that he himself when he got out and
was to take horse again to be gone was fain to hang a quarter of an
hour upon the neck of his horse weeping, before he had the power to
mount, so strange an impression was there upon him and generally
upon the people upon having been thus expostulated with for neglect
of the Bible.' No one who is intimate with the sermons of the
Puritan divines needs to be protected from the oft-recurring charge
that they were fanatical and 'abandoned' in their preaching, but
we do well to remember, on the other hand, that an absence of
emotion and a coldness in delivery was no mark of their pulpits.
Rogers is singular by any standards, yet he was revealing a fervour
and an imaginativeness that was not at all untypical of his fellow
Puritans in the pulpit.

It is worthwhile to recall one other incident relating to John
Rogers of Dedham. It is related by yet another Puritan, Giles
Firmin, author of the famous *Real Christian*. He tells of an occasion
in his youth when he arrived late with some other youths for the
service in Rogers' church. Rogers, observing the slight commotion
as they pressed into the crowded congregation, cried out from the
pulpit with his usual mixture of bluff heartiness and real solemnity,
'Here are some young ones for Christ. Will nothing serve you but
you must have Christ? Then you shall have him' – and so continued his sermon. This made such a deep and lasting impression
upon the young Firmin's mind that he later dated his conversion
from this time.

Richard Sibbes (1577-1635)

It were presumptuous to dismiss in a few lines as we have to here the worth of the 'heavenly' Richard Sibbes, that 'English Leighton' as he was described. Sibbes, more than any other of his time was a second Perkins in his influence with the rising generation of Puritans of his day. More urbane and polished in his preaching than Rogers of Dedham, his preaching was not less cosmopolitan – indeed it was even more so – attracting as it did both the high and low. His teaching was full and expository in the best Puritan tradition, his style clear and winsome, his mind broad and cultured and his piety uncompromising and practical. His books, especially the far-famed *Bruised Reed* and *The Soul's Conflict*, were immensely popular among all classes and were a great power for good in dealing with troubled consciences and convicted souls.

First lecturer and later vicar of Trinity Church, Cambridge, his rising fame took him in 1618, despite troubles arising from his 'Puritanism', to Gray's Inn, London as 'preacher' there. This position he occupied until his death, though he accepted along with this the mastership of St. Catherine's at his old university. From the students of Cambridge, many of whom were destined to be numbered among the 'great ones' of their age, to his incomparable auditory of Puritan nobility in London, he maintained an unfailing and potent influence for the Puritan cause. An old Puritan, Zechary Catlin, spoke for many when he said of Sibbes in reference to his preaching, 'No man that ever I was acquainted withal got so far into my heart or lay so close therein'.

Richard Baxter (1615-1691)

One of the most popular and prolific Puritan preachers and authors, Baxter was possibly also one of the most winsome and romantic figures on the Puritan scene. He was certainly one of the most redoubtable. No marked honours of State or Church fell to him; he was a pastor, preacher and writer whose influence owed nothing to preferment from Parliament or Church. Daringly independent in all that he did, said or believed, his theological writings as often provoked his compeers to exasperation as admiration. Yet, his moving spirit was not revolutionary but pacific. His breadth of genius and catholicity of spirit are well known and observable in his one hundred and forty literary productions, which range from learned Latin or English treatises to simple catechisms for families and the most detailed practical 'directories' for Christian living. His ministerial life at Kidderminster, stretching over fifteen years, has stood for three centuries as a model of the pastoral and preaching office, and his life and labours through over fifty years of ministry undertaken in constant pain and with incredible diligence, secure for him an unrivalled place in the history of English Nonconformity. His preaching style, markedly forceful, unadorned and compelling, always had a very potent evangelistic emphasis and his books on conversion, such as the famous *Call to the Unconverted* went through a legendary number of editions. His fellow Puritan, Thomas Manton, considered him 'one of the most extraordinary persons the Christian Church had produced since the apostles' days', adding that he, Manton, 'did not look upon himself as worthy to carry his books after him'. The nineteenth-century antiquarian and Puritan scholar, Alexander Balloch Grosart, once said in a lecture on Baxter that he 'drew more hearts to the great Broken Heart than any single Englishman of his age', and after a review of his achievements declared roundly that he was 'awed at the quantity of *being* in him'.

Jeremiah Burroughs (1599-1646)

Burroughs was educated at Emmanuel College, Cambridge, but was obliged to leave the university, and afterward the country, on account of his Nonconformity. After a period as colleague to Edmund Calamy at St. Edmunds, he enjoyed a five-year lectureship in Tivetshall, Norfolk. The infamous 'articles' of Bishop Wren in 1636 led to his suspension and his being deprived of his living, and after a short time under the hospitality of that great Puritan nobleman, the Earl of Warwick, he received a call from the English Congregational Church at Rotterdam, Holland, to become 'teacher' of the Church where William Ames had ministered under similar conditions. He returned to England after the outbreak of the Civil War and was chosen as preacher to the 'two largest congregations in the land' – at Stepney and Cripplegate in London. In the four years that followed, before his death at forty-seven, Burroughs preached inexhaustibly and wrote prolifically. He exercised a lasting influence on the Church-government controversies of the day, both by his firm stand for independency and the irenic nature of that stand. In some respects his sermons, as those of Manton, more nearly approach the modern ideal of sermon presentation than many of that age. In their style and substance there is nothing redundant or extravagant; hardly is there a word out of place and they proceed with entire adequacy and perfect

proportion to prove, illustrate and drive home their doctrines. At
any rate, Thomas Brooks was glad to write a recommendatory
preface to a posthumous treatise of 'that prince of preachers, Mr.
Jeremiah Burroughs, who is now a shining sun in the upper world'.

Thomas Manton (1620-1677)

Manton seems to have united the advantage of nature, circumstances
and grace from his youth. Child of the manse and youthful
graduate of Wadham College, Oxford, he was ordained at twenty by
the famous Joseph Hall, Bishop of Exeter (later of Norwich).
Three years' ministry in Devon succeeded this prestigious beginning
and at the end of that period the patronage of Colonel Popham
obtained for him a living at Stoke Newington. It was from here
that he began to attract the notice of the London clergy and even
Parliament. Seven years later, Manton succeeded the aged
Puritan rector of Covent Garden, Obadiah Sedgwick (he was the
only person the old Puritan would even hear of as a successor) and
thereafter held a prominent position in the metropolis to the end of
his life.

A presbyterian, he was infinitely more peace-loving than many of
his fellows; perhaps the most unwise thing he ever did was to play a
large part in the restoration of Charles II. This did not save him
from becoming a frequent sufferer for his Nonconformity, though his
generous spirit always held the respect of many who opposed his
beloved Puritanism.

His great love and work was preaching, and though he preached
three or four times a week for many years to large and discerning
congregations, yet William Bates, that most classic and cultured of
the later Puritan preachers says, he 'never heard him preach a mean
sermon'. This was the result of much labour as well as natural
gifts and true devotion on Manton's part. He was 'tireless' in both
preaching and the preparation of his sermons. Often, he would rise
up from bed in the dead of night eager to pen some new idea for the
sermon in hand, and would write at length. His sermons fill twenty
out of the twenty-two volumes of his works in their nineteenth
century edition, and they range from his famous series of one
hundred and seventy-six sermons on Psalm 119 to single sermons on
various occasions. His famous contemporary, Archbishop Ussher,
used to say that Manton was one of the 'best preachers in England'
and Stephen Charnock thought him 'the best collector of sense of

the age' – a reference to the well-researched content of Manton's productions. It is the measure of the man's humility that he published in his lifetime only his expositions upon James and Jude and a handful of sermons, leaving the vast majority of his manuscripts to the will of Providence after his death.

Much the same could be said of Manton's sermons as was said of Burroughs'. Both reflect the Puritan preaching at its very best and with few of the blemishes characteristic of the age in its literature and public speech.

John Owen (1616-1683)

A man who can produce more than four-score written works, several of them large folios, and all of them weighty with learning and significance for the age is a mighty theologian, and a man who can command an auditory of two-thousand weekly in his early thirties is no mean preacher. Both of these did John Owen, who shares with Thomas Goodwin the distinction of being one of the foremost Independents of his day and one of the greatest theologians of all time. The theologian redoubtably (and many have said irrefutably) championed all the traditional Protestant tenets of Calvin and the Reformation, and the preacher produced weighty quartos of superb practical divinity and devotion.

Owen's career led him from the obscurity of a small Essex living to the Vice-chancellorship of Oxford University, becoming by stages between the two, chaplain to Oliver Cromwell in Ireland and Scotland, and Dean of Christ Church, Oxford. The death of Cromwell swiftly altered events and the years that followed this and the subsequent Restoration were, for Owen, largely years of retirement from public affairs. But they were also years in which, as a London pastor and preacher, Owen's literary output increased and with it came an unquestionable influence upon contemporary and later Protestant Nonconformity.

Thomas Goodwin (1600-1680)

Born in Norfolk in 1600, strong religious tendencies in the boy Goodwin passed over into equally strong ambitious ones in the young man and student. While studying for 'the Church' at this time he was consumed with a desire to become a great orator rather than a great Christian and minister. His conversion at twenty produced right priorities in this as in all else and goes far to explain why his style throughout his life remained studiously free of oratorical ornament – even perhaps to the point of occasional dryness.

Goodwin became fellow of St. Catherine's, Cambridge and lecturer of Trinity Church, but was from the beginning, suspected because of his Nonconformist leanings and in 1634 he resigned amidst increasing pressures from 'the Prelatic party', and spent the next five years consolidating his Congregational convictions. In 1639, as Calamy puts it, 'the persecution growing hot in England he went into Holland . . . to enjoy liberty of conscience and settled as pastor of the English Church at Arnheim.' He returned to London at the beginning of the Long Parliament and formed a gathered Church in the metropolis. During the ten years of this pastorate, Goodwin rose to eminence as a preacher. He was appointed a member of the Westminster Assembly where his brilliance made him the acknowledged leader of the 'dissenting brethren' of Independents and a prominent figure in Assembly debates.

In 1650, Parliament appointed him President of Magdalen College, Oxford. Goodwin's breadth as well as depth of learning, together with his deep desire to train young men for the ministry, made him eminently suitable for such a position. One of the more notable results of the prosperity of the Independents under the protection of Cromwell was the Savoy conference, at which Goodwin was one of the most prominent members, and at the behest of which he took a major part (with Owen, Bridge, Caryl and others) in composing the Savoy Declaration – 'the first and basic English Congregational [or Independent] statement of doctrine and Church polity'.

The Restoration saw the end of his Oxford career and his removal from Oxford to London, where many members of the gathered church which he had founded at Oxford joined him. As pastor of this church, Goodwin's life passed quietly enough for its remaining twenty years. He continued to write learnedly and prolifically and to preach systematically. His preaching, while very plain, is redeemed from tediousness by the quality of its matter and the deep sensitivity of its thinking. A massive theologian and a true biblicist, there was yet a streak of something approaching mysticism in his nature which lent him rare insights into Scripture and the devout life and which to this day makes his writings as warm as they are instructive.

Christopher Love (1618-1651)

Christopher Love enjoyed a short-lived but extremely popular ministry at St. Lawrence Jewry and St. Anne's Aldersgate, London. Though a zealous Presbyterian in matters of Church government, his preaching was broad-based and eminently practical. As the various volumes of his sermons show, his preaching gathered up much that was representative of Puritanism at its best and most popular. His untimely death is responsible for both his fame and his neglect. Political naivete, which had on more than one occasion marred his reputation, cast its deepest shadow when it brought about his death by execution for his part in a plot (involving several other Puritan ministers) to restore Charles II. Notwithstanding the unpropitious circumstances, Thomas Manton preached his funeral sermon and showed the esteem in which Christopher Love was held by his fellow Puritan ministers and people. It is a tragedy that the sermons of a man who ranks with Brooks, Watson, Manton and Burroughs in the foremost phalanx of powerful and popular preachers of Commonwealth London should have been neglected and remain out of print.

Thomas Brooks (c.1608-1680)

Almost nothing is known about the personal life of Brooks but of his public popularity there can be no doubt. From the pulpit of St. Thomas Apostle's and St. Margaret's, Fish Street Hill, London, his fame as a preacher rivalled that of any of his brethren. If illustrations are the windows of a sermon, Thomas Brooks must have been the master-glazier of his period. His works are a veritable Crystal Palace of illuminating anecdotes and figures of speech. His rich prose and racy anecdotal style frequently obscure a learning which he most certainly had but never loved to display. Says a fellow minister and friend of Brooks: 'He had a body of divinity in his head and the power of it in his heart,' and, we may add, in his books too. His fertility of mind is constantly spilling-over into the margins of his books – all of which derive from material preached before publication. Many of his works passed into almost as many editions as there are errata in the hurriedly turned-out copies. There was no more popular preacher in the London of Cromwell and the Interregnum than Thomas Brooks.

William Bridge (1600-1670)

Fellow of Emmanuel College, Cambridge and a life-long scholar
(seventeen hours' study a day was commonplace with him), William
Bridge played his own part – and not a mean one either – in the
development of Nonconformity. From 1631 to 1636 he was lecturer, first in Colchester, Essex, and then in Norwich. Upon his
deprivation by Wren and that implacable prelate's insistence upon
his excommunication and arrest, Bridge fled to Holland and became
one of the pastors of the English gathered church at Rotterdam.
In 1642, under the new order of things, Bridge returned to England
where, in the following year he settled at Yarmouth as town
'preacher' and pastor to the newly gathered Congregational church
there (many of which were of his old flock at Norwich). During his
seventeen years there Bridge was both active and prominent, first as
one of the famous Independents at the Assembly of Divines at
Westminster and later as one of the most prominent members of the
Savoy Conference.

After his deprivation, in 1661, of his Yarmouth post, we learn
little of his course until his death in 1670. He remained in Yarmouth
until 1663, spent the following four or five years preaching in the
South (in Clapham, Surrey, according to Wood) and returned to
Yarmouth for the last two or three years of his life. Many of his
numerous writings were published during his life-time by fellow-
Puritans and more after his death. They are devout, lively,
practical and full of sound doctrine. His style is somewhat like
that of Burroughs and Manton, eminently readable, and his works
are among the very best of practical Puritan writings.

Richard Gilpin (1625-1700)

Richard Gilpin was a doctor of bodies as well as souls, a man of
culture and talent who united grace with nature to become one of
the most revered figures in Puritanism in the North of England.
He was born of an old and prosperous Westmorland family, though
little is known of his early life. It appears that he studied first
medicine and then theology, succeeding by turns to pastorates in
Durham and London (where he was assistant to Dr. Wilkins, later
to become Bishop of Chester). From here, in 1652 or 1653, he was
presented with the ample benefice of Greystoke in Cumberland.
Here he was to remain as rector until shortly before the Great

Ejection of 1662 when, with so many others of his fellow-Puritans, he 'lost a good living to keep a good conscience'.

He was not long in this state of retirement before the King, Charles II, offered him as 'a person highly esteemed in the North of England' the Bishopric of Carlisle. This attempt to buy off some of the leading Puritans, and so lower the profile of a situation which involved the mass departure of almost two thousand of the National Church's best men, extended to such other eminent Puritans as Richard Baxter, Edmund Calamy (senior) and others. That Gilpin is included is evidence, from an unexpected direction, of his position and influence among the Nonconforming brotherhood.

In the reconstruction of things which followed the Ejection, large numbers of Nonconforming 'meeting houses' appeared, in which met congregations which had formed themselves into churches, quite distinct from the local parish church. Among others, a large congregation of Nonconformists united at Newcastle, where they built a fine large chapel. In 1668-1669 this church invited Richard Gilpin to become its minister and for the remaining thirty-two years of his life he remained in this charge. From the beginning of this ministry, his outstanding abilities and peaceable spirit held together a large and diverse congregation.

In 1676 Gilpin paid a brief visit to Leyden, Holland where he obtained his long deferred M.D. A year later, in 1677, appeared his most famous work, the *Daemonologia Sacra, or a Treatise of Satan's Temptations*. This work gathered up much that was finest in his own ministry and in that of the Puritanism which he represented. It immediately obtained a place in the first rank of Nonconformist works of the day, and, as its reprintings in both the eighteenth and nineteenth centuries suggest, remained in just celebrity long after.

Something should also be said about *a few of the lesser-known names which appear in the succeeding pages*, names such as Matthew Lawrence, Joseph Symonds and John Wells, to mention but three. It may appear surprising that these names should be appended to any list of great preachers of the period. Yet, had Puritan England not been almost prodigal of great preaching their names and careers would not have been almost entirely forgotten to posterity as they have been. Even so, they are only the tip of the iceberg. The truth is that very very many old and long-forgotten books, quartos, octavos and duodecimos are available to the researcher of Puritan preaching which had only one printing and of which few copies were 'turned off'. These were the pulpit and literary productions of obscure country preachers, which reveal a most compelling and spiritual pulpit ministry.   In a less richly endowed age such men would have gained note as among the best preachers of their day.

Matthew Lawrence (1600-1653/4)

Of Lawrence's earlier life and ministry we know nothing, but he became prominent as a successor of the famous Samuel Ward at Ipswich, Suffolk where he was town preacher at the Church of St. Mary le Tower.   For nine years, from 1643 or 1644 to his death, Lawrence held this position with the unabated esteem of the town Corporation and people.   Perhaps it should be remembered that, at this time, Ipswich was a place of considerable importance as the capital town of one of the most populous and wealthy counties in England.   Ipswich as a centre of commerce and civilisation should therefore be thought of much as Manchester, Birmingham or Bristol would be today.   Further, it was a leading stronghold of Puritanism, with a redoubtable history of Nonconformity stretching back to Elizabeth I and Whitgift's day.   For instance, sixty Suffolk ministers were ejected in 1583/4 and nearly one hundred in 1662, and over this period Suffolk had produced some of the most eminent of the Puritan divines.

Of such a county and of such a character was Ipswich, which could boast a galaxy of Puritan divines on its own account.   It was in the midst of such burning and shining lights that Matthew Lawrence shone with a lustre of his own.   A little of his character and ministry is glimpsed in the references to him by his editors, writing in the preface of his posthumous book.   He was, they write, 'a mighty Apollos in the sacred Scriptures, so abundant in alleging apt and clear Scriptures for grounds and enlargements that he might be called, as another once was, "the Ark of the Scriptures" '.   They continue: 'His life and disposition was made up of a meek and quiet spirit, a melting heart toward God and a healing, closing [reconciling] spirit toward his brethren though in some things dissenting.' They conclude: 'Such low spirits are fitted to receive the high revelations of faith and living by it.'

Of Lawrence's private life and background scarcely anything is known.   He was of a Lincolnshire family, and as a curious comment on the shortness of life in those days it may be observed that his first wife married him as her third husband and his second wife as her second.   Lawrence died aged fifty-three years.   His one book,

John Rogers Preacher of the word of God 31
at Dedham in Essex..

*John Rogers of Dedham!   A name to conjure with in
seventeenth century Essex, especially amongst young men.
Preacher extraordinary and a fervent soul-winner he is as far
removed as possible from the dreary word-spinner and hair-
splitter which is the popular myth about the Puritans.*

Loe here the Glorie of the slighted Gowne!
Who was to's Tribe an ornament and Crowne!
Who, with vast Learning and well-study'd Youth
Had pious Age, soe knew and loud the Truth.
The Graver shews his Face, but if you'd looke
Into his Minde, 'tis pictur'd in this booke:
By wch his Name will liue, till Time shall lye
Rould in Æternity; and Death shall Dye.

William Gouge (1575-1653). *Revered and persecuted by turns
as an 'Arch-Puritan' he ministered for 45 years to one of the largest
and most influential congregations in London. To speak of his
celebrated series of sermons lasting 33 years on the epistle to the
Hebrews is to offer a glimpse of the magnitude of the Puritan
pulpit in 17th Century England.*

The Use and Practice of Faith, comprehensive in its treatment, sage in its counsel and full of the 'life' of the Puritan pulpit, is not inferior to any of the Puritan treatises extant on faith.

Joseph Symonds (d.1652)

It is not known when Symonds was born, though his death may be fixed from a letter to Richard Baxter from Dr. Thomas Doolittle where it appears that Symonds died in Essex in 1652. As a young man he had been an assistant to the famous Puritan Thomas Gataker at Rotherhithe near London, but in 1632 became rector of St. Martin's, Ironmonger's Lane, in the metropolis. Six or seven years later he resigned this living, seceded from the National Church and became an Independent, leaving England for Holland. At Rotterdam, Symonds was chosen as pastor to the English church, along with William Bridge who fulfilled the same role, and Jeremiah Burroughs who was lecturer to the church. Here he remained, probably for about seven years, though sometimes returning to England to preach to Parliament. In 1647 Symonds became Fellow of Eton College and was Vice-President of that historic school. As his Fellowship terminated on the 17th October, 1652, this may well have been the exact date of his death.

His *Case and Cure of a deserted soul*, so much quoted in this book, shows a mind and heart replete with the best qualities of Puritan learning and devotion.

John Wells (d.1676)

Of John Wells even less is known. A Fellow of St. John's College, Oxford he was, before his ejection, minister at St. Olave, Jewry, in London. From a funeral sermon at his death we learn that, 'his preaching was plain and profitable, suitable to the capacities of his auditory. He was of an affable disposition; of such candour and ingenuity as to win the affections of many. In him grace and good nature met. He was of a forgiving spirit. Kindness made a lasting impression upon him, but injuries he forgot. He was very charitable to the poor many of whom were both clothed and fed by his liberality'. That he was invited to preach two of the famous sermons now called *The Cripplegate Exercises* is sufficient indication that he was held in respect by his fellow-Puritans.

From his thick quarto on practical godliness, *The Practical Sabbatarian*, quoted further on in this book, it really is a wonder that Wells is not better known. His rich blend of doctrine and application, his wise counsel and lively style, his power of strong argument and melting pathos suggest him to have been, in the pulpit and the study, representative of all that was fine in Puritanism.

Of course, this is only a tithe of the number of truly great preachers in the Nonconformist ranks between the reigns of Elizabeth I and James II, and other names clamour for attention such as those of John Cotton, Paul Baine, William Gouge, John Howe, John Preston, Watson, Hildersham, Byfield, Sedgwick, Clarkson, Charnock and many more. The fact that the catalogue of names mentioned spans a hundred years is itself eloquent. It is due to no lack of historical sense or precision that, in many treatments of Puritan thought and preaching, Puritans several generations apart in time are spoken of and quoted in one breath. It is part of the phenomenon of Puritanism that in its basic and distinctive features it was stable and consistent through generations, and while we see healthy development throughout this time, especially in ecclesiology, yet it is not such a great step from Perkins to Traill or from Bates to Baxter.

What is more, the doctrines, practice and standards of living and preaching were much the same wherever the Puritan spirit was found, and while multitudes of country ministers were less talented than some of their more famous brethren, yet it is undeniable that an even, basic *quality* pervades the record of Puritan ministries which we have. Take it at its most *average* and the overall Puritan preaching challenges ministers of our own day to do as well, and insists that we *may* do as well with comparable (and attainable) diligence and devotion. It is the genius of the Puritan pulpit that it is the contemporary of every age in what it teaches and in what it inspires.

THE PURITAN PREACHING

1. *The Dignity of Preaching*

'Christ asked his disciples what they thought of him, Matt. 16:13,' writes Henry Smith, himself the most popular preacher of his day. 'So,' he continues, 'I would ask you, what do you think of preachers? Is he a contemptible person which bringeth the message of God; which hath the name of an Angel (2 Cor. 5:20), and all his words are messengers of life? . . . Prophets are of such account with God, that it is said, Amos 3:7: God will do nothing before he reveals it unto his prophets; so prophets are, as it were, God's counsellors.'[1]

John Mayer replies to a Puritan's question with a Puritan's answer when he writes:

> He that is sent of God to preach, speaketh in his name, and what he saith is as if God from heaven spoke it . . . our saviour Christ therefore saith to his disciples going forth to preach, 'he that heareth you, heareth me, and he that despiseth you, despiseth me' . . . so every preacher of the word speaketh only what God putteth into his mouth whilst he keepeth him to preaching according to the Word. And therefore St. Paul commendeth the Thessalonians, for they received his preaching as God's Word, such as indeed it was (1 Thess. 2:13).[2]

The Puritan preachers' obvious pride in their high and holy office is reflected even in the title pages of many of their books. You will look in vain, for instance, for any record of academic distinction after the name of Thomas Brooks. As A. B. Grosart, speaking of Brooks' years at Emmanuel College, Cambridge observes: 'In all likelihood he proceeded from degree to degree although in common with other of the Puritans, he places none on his title pages, preferring the nobler designation "Preacher of the Gospel" or "Preacher of the Word".'[3]

Nor is it surprising that they gloried in a title which had been so honoured in the world's history: they were very conscious of that spiritual pedigree to which Edward Reynolds referred when he spoke of 'the dignity and excellence of this office which not only the holy prophets and apostles did attend upon . . . but the blessed angels. . . . Yea, he who is the "Lord of Angels", was solemnly anointed unto this function, to preach the acceptable year of the Lord . . . and though he were the Lord of life and glory, unto whom every knee must bow . . . yet he did not disdain to be a minister . . . and to go about preaching the gospel of the kingdom' (Matt. 4:23).[4]

Arthur Hildersham expounds and applies this last observation when he writes:

> Preaching was the chief work of all that Christ, the chief pastor, was sent to do in his ministry. Luke 4:18,43 . . . neither was there any one work of his calling that he did so much and so diligently exercise himself in as in preaching . . . Christ sent me, saith the apostle, 1 Cor. 1:17, not to baptise (that is not so much to baptise) but to preach the gospel . . . and this is the chief work that we are called of God to exercise ourselves in . . . gladly taking all opportunities for doing this work.[5]

It is important to observe in that extract how easily Hildersham slides over from the preaching of Christ to the preaching of the

apostle, and thence to all ministers of the gospel.   Another Puritan,
Paul Baine, shows us how correct this is when he observes from
Paul's words to the Church in Ephesus (which our Lord in person
never visited while on earth), 'And he came and preached peace to
you who were far off and peace to those who were near', Eph. 2:17:
'He saith *Christ* preached to them. . . .   Now he was never a minister
but of the circumcision (Rom. 15:8), to the lost sheep of the house of
Israel (Matt. 15:24) in his own person.   Therefore we see that
Christ is present and hath a part in preaching even when *men* preach
("ye seek a proof of Christ speaking in me", 2 Cor. 13:3) . . . for
this is the office of Christ our great Prophet, not only in his own
Person to open to us the will of his Father . . . but to be present and
teach inwardly in the heart with that Word which is outwardly
sounded unto the ear by men. . . .   Thus Paul preached to the ear,
but Christ to the heart of Lydia.   This must teach us to look upon
Christ as the chief Prophet among us, and the chief Preacher who-
soever speaketh.'[6]

Richard Sibbes is just as enthusiastic in his elevation of the
preaching office:

> Christ, when he ascended on high and led captivity captive (he
> would give no mean gift then, when he was to ascend triumphantly
> to heaven) the greatest gift he could give was 'some to be prophets,
> some apostles, some teachers (and preachers) for the building up of
> the body of Christ till we all meet, a perfect man in Christ'.   'I will
> send them pastors according to my own heart' saith God (Jer. 3:15).
> It is the gift of all gifts, the ordinance of preaching.   God esteems it
> so, Christ esteems it so, and so should we esteem it.[7]

Certainly the Puritan brotherhood fulfilled Sibbes' charge, and
Nehemiah Rogers in an instructive and interesting survey gathers
together the many titles of honour which the Scriptures give to
faithful preachers:

> The great benefit we have by the Word preached, few do or indeed
> can conceive; and therefore the Lord doth teach it us by sundry
> comparisons and similitudes such as every man can understand and
> judge of.   Sometimes God's people are called the Lord's *building*,
> his *house* and *temple*, as 1 Cor. 3:9 and 2 Cor. 6:16, and preachers
> resembled to *builders* and *carpenters*, who must both lay the foundation
> and set up the frame, 1 Cor. 3:10.   Sometimes God's people are
> called God's *household*, Gal. 6:10, Eph. 2:19; and then the Ministers
> of God's Word are resembled to *stewards*, who must give every one
> their portion of meat in due season, Luke 12:42.   Sometimes the
> godly are called the *sons and daughters of God*, as 2 Cor. 6:18, and then
> preachers are called both spiritual *fathers*, by whom they are begotten
> unto God, 1 Cor. 4:15, and spiritual *mothers*, who travail in birth
> with them, Gal. 4:19, and *nurses*, by whom they are fed while they

are babes in Christ, 1 Thess. 2:7. Sometimes the people are called
the Lord's pleasant *garden* and fruitful *orchard*, Cant. 4:12,13; and
then ministers are called the *planters* and *waterers* of it, 1 Cor. 3:6.
Sometimes the church is called the Lord's *husbandry* (cultivated soil)
and *cornfield*, 1 Cor. 3:9, and then we are called both his *labourers*,
who by stubbing, dunging and ploughing, must prepare it, 1 Cor.
3:9; and his *seedsmen* who are to sow it, Mark 4:26; as also his *reapers*,
who must get the corn down, and bring it into his barn, John 4:38.
Sometimes the people are called *pilgrims*, who travel in a way unknown and dangerous, 1 Pet. 2:11, and then are we ministers com-
pared to *guides*, Heb. 3:7 and unto *lights*, Matt. 5:14, because we light
this candle and hold it forth to direct you in the ways of life.[8]

By this time it will be clear that wherever Puritanism was strong,
the Puritan pulpit was very much in evidence, and the office of
preacher and teacher was elevated to a place of dignity and prominence. From what did preaching derive its honour and dignity?
The answer which was common to all who were Puritan in their
thinking was plain, as we shall see. Godward, preaching derived
its honour from that seal which God had placed upon it by which
it was endowed with particular spiritual potency for the conversion
of men and their building up in the faith; manward, its dignity
was increased by the human need for it, to inspire, instruct, warn,
rebuke and comfort. We turn, then, to consider the Puritan
emphasis on the *necessity* of a preaching ministry.

2. *The Necessity of Preaching*

(a) With regard to the integrity of the ministry
In the fresh morning of Elizabethan Puritanism, William Perkins
informed his Cambridge auditory, a rising generation of Puritans,
that preaching was 'the principal duty of a minister'.[9] Later, in
the late evening of the Puritan age, Robert Traill, in a sermon
entitled *By what means may ministers best win souls?* almost repeats
Perkins' very words when he says that 'the principal work of a
minister is preaching; the principal benefit people have by them is to
hear the Lord's word from them'.[10]

Throughout the long intervening years, whether within the sound
of musketry and cannon, or to a crowded Parliament, or in the
cramped cellar of a private house in forbidden and forbidding times,
the Puritan preachers lived and loved their 'principal duty' and
preached on – a race of preachers whose teaching lived long after
they themselves ceased from their labours.

They would never have allowed that minimising of the place of
the pulpit which is so common in our own day. The elevation of
even the pastoral office above the preaching of the Word of God
would have been unthinkable for them. The gift of preaching and
its faithful and diligent exercise was something for which, to the
Puritan mind, there was no substitute. 'They therefore,' warns
William Perkins:

> are thoroughly deceived who think a minister to discharge
> sufficiently his duty though he preach not, if he keep good hospitality
> and make peace among his neighbours and perform other works of
> charity and good life: for if a minister have not this virtue [of preach-
> ing] he hath none. . . .[11]

Turning to the middle period of English Puritanism, we have
already seen Arthur Hildersham inculcate preaching as 'the chief
work that we are called of God to exercise ourselves in', and have
heard Sibbes characterise it as 'the gift of all gifts'. Therefore, we
are not surprised to hear Thomas Hall insist that 'ministers must be
preachers . . . not only they may but they *must* preach. There is
a necessity backed with a woe (1 Cor. 9:16). So that they must
either preach or perish: this must be done or they are undone'.[12]

Edward Reynolds, in his quiet, thorough way, presses home the
lesson. The preaching of the gospel, he says:

> is necessary . . . as in a special manner appointed by Christ, who
> is the King and Lawgiver in his Church. As his Father sent him,
> and gave him a commission and a command to discharge the
> service which was entrusted in his hand; which, he, with all willing-
> ness and obedience set about, though it were not only to preaching
> but to dying, that so the pleasure of the Lord might prosper in his
> hand; even so did he send forth his disciples with a strict commission
> and command (as having all power in heaven and earth given to
> him) to preach the gospel (Matt. 28:18-20). And in order to the
> perpetual discharge of that service, he appointed . . . pastors and
> teachers to attend the same to the world's end, for the perfecting of
> the saints, for the work of the ministry, for the building up of the
> body of Christ (Eph. 4:13). And accordingly the apostles took
> special care to commit the same service unto faithful men, who
> might be able to teach others, and appointed elders to be ordained
> in every city for the carrying on of this work (Acts 14:23; 2 Tim. 2:2;
> Titus 1:5). And as our Saviour, by the argument drawn from his
> power over them, and their love to him, presseth the exercise of this
> duty upon his disciples (Matt. 28:18,19; John 21:15-17), so do the
> apostles afterward, by the Author of their superintendence, the Holy
> Spirit; by the property of God in his Church; by the blood whereby
> it was purchased (Acts 20:28); by the presence of God; by the
> judgement to come (2 Tim. 4:1); by the crown of glory which they
> shall receive from the Chief Shepherd (1 Pet. 5:1-4), press diligence

and fidelity in the same upon those whom they ordained thereunto.[13]

All of this brings us back to Traill, who, at the close of the era, sums up the Puritan unity on this point with the conclusion: 'Art thou a minister? Thou must be a preacher. An unpreaching minister is a sort of contradiction.'[14]

(b) With regard to the salvation of the elect

It will further be realised just why the Puritans so elevated preaching as the chief work and glory of the ministry, when we consider John Downame's representative statement, that preaching is 'God's own ordinance which he hath instituted and ordained for the gathering of the saints, and building the body of his Church, as appeareth Eph. 4:11,12. Neither doth he use ordinarily, any other means (especially where this is to be had) for the true conversion of his children, and for the working of the sanctifying graces of his Spirit in them'.[15] Not that preaching was thought to be the exclusive means of saving men, but it was considered that God had ordained it to be the principal and settled means of gathering his Church. Thus John Mayer tells us: 'The preaching of the Word of God is the means whereby God begetteth us again . . . nothing is more common than to set forth the Word of God as the means of our conversion, faith and salvation (Rom. 10:14; 1:16; 1 Cor. 1:21; 1 Pet. 1:23; Matt. 13).'[16]

Thomas White, in a Cripplegate Exercise lecture on *Effectual Calling*, could recite to an approving audience of fellow-Puritans, as a universal dictum of the movement, that: 'The most ordinary means of our effectual calling is the preaching of the Word . . . and though by other means men *may* be called, yet seldom or never any are called that neglect and condemn this.'[17] We are prepared, therefore, to read from Elnathan Parr's commentary on Romans: 'Without the preaching of the gospel, there is (ordinarily) no salvation. The gospel is the power of God unto salvation, not written in leaves, but preached (Rom. 1:16; 1 Cor. 1:21; Jas. 1:18).'[18] Perhaps we shall not, in consequence, find too abrupt his answer to the question he catechetically puts forward: 'Shall none be saved, but those which hear sermons? Answer: No, ordinarily.'

No one has written to better effect, in giving reasons for the doctrine that the preaching of the gospel is God's great converting ordinance, than Thomas Goodwin. He begins:

1. It is so appointed and ordained by God . . . (Is. 55:10,11) . . .
2. As God appointed it, so Christ prayed for it . . . (John 17:19, 20) . . .
3. As God the Father appointed it, and God the Son prayed for it,

so God the Holy Spirit is, by promise and covenant engaged to
accompany it with his blessing unto the seed of Christ for ever
(Is. 59:21).[19]

Goodwin then deals in detail with his point in replying to supposed
objections.   In answer to the question, 'Why has God chosen the
preaching of the Word by men to be the principal means of converting sinners?' he states, firstly, that God chooses thus to work
mediately rather than immediately, both to 'shew his divers manner
of working, for he still loves to vary his dispensations toward man'
and 'to hide' his Word and working 'from the eyes of the undiscern-
ing world who contemn the means to their destruction'.   Secondly,
God has chosen the preaching of the Word to fulfil his saving
purposes among and toward his elect, 'because it is the weakest
means of all others, and therefore his power would the more appear
unto his own glory in it', and he has chosen to reveal himself by
'this most simple and naked representation' rather than by any other
visible means, because 'the word was less apt to be abused to
idolatry'.   Thirdly, Goodwin insists that it is hearing the Word
preached, rather than reading the Word written that converts,
because 'the simplest can ordinarily hear as well as the wisest, and
so the poor do come and receive the gospel who otherwise would
want [lack] it'.   Fourthly, preachers become the vehicle of this
ordinance when they expound (Neh. 8:7,8) rather than merely read
aloud the Scriptures, both 'because of the dullness that there is in
many people' (Acts 8:30; Ezra 7:10), and 'because Jesus Christ,
when he ascended, gave gifts unto men (Eph. 4:8). . . . As he left
the word written behind him, so he gave gifts unto men to expound
it, both for the begetting and perfecting of the saints.   Now as for
reading the word, everyone can do that, but an "interpreter" is
"one of a thousand" (Job. 33:23).'[20]   Furthermore, as Goodwin
points out significantly, 'it is not the letter of the word that ordinarily
doth convert, but the spiritual meaning of it as revealed and expounded'.   Lastly, Goodwin asserts the reasons why God chooses
'mere men' to preach his word rather than himself or angels doing
so:

1. Because men themselves first chose this way, as most agreeable
   and suitable to themselves and unto their natures and conditions.
   Deut. 5:25,26: 'If we hear the voice of the Lord our God we shall
   die.   Go thou therefore near, and hear all that the Lord our God
   shall say, and come and speak unto us and we will hear it' . . . and
   God hearing the people say this, said unto Moses, 'They have well
   spoken . . . stand thou therefore here, and I will speak to thee all
   the statutes and judgements which thou shalt teach them . . .'.

2. God betrusted this treasure in earthen vessels, not heavenly (as it
is 2 Cor. 4:7) because we are not able to behold the angels. You
see how sons of men have always trembled when they appeared.
And further, we should have been apt to worship them, as John
would have done, Rev. 22:8; and therefore God appointed men like
ourselves to be the instruments.

No Puritan reasoning is complete without its application and
John Mayer makes 'use' of all this when he warmly exhorts his
people: 'Learn we from hence to have the preaching of the Word,
and to have desire to hear it as often as we can: for hereby grace is
wrought in our hearts, the defaced image of God, which is righteousness and holiness is repaired, and we are translated from the state
of Satan's slaves, to the state of God's children who shall inherit
his earthly kingdom.'[21]

Perhaps we should give the last word on this matter to Nehemiah
Rogers, who, with a flash of typical Puritan quaintness concludes:
'Let these considerations prevail with us not to slight the means
because they are but weak, and like Ebed-Melech's rags (Jer. 38:11),
of themselves worthless; seeing by God's good grace and wise dispensation they are let down to draw us out of the dungeon of sin and
misery wherein we stick, and are ever followed upon the conscionable
use with blessed deliverance! Therefore as Jeremiah did by those,
so let us by these: let us put them under our arm-holes!'[22]

(c) With regard to the building up of the saints

It is not to be thought for all this that the preacher's work ends in
the conversion of his hearers: 'For we must consider,' insists the
venerable Richard Rogers of Wethersfield:

that God hath appointed this preaching of his Word to perfect the
faith of his elect (1 Pet. 5:2) . . . First . . . they are cleansed from
error and darkness about religion and manners . . . and grow more
sound in the knowledge of the truth, and see more particularly into
the way and whole course of Christianity. . . . Again, this quickeneth
them in their drowsiness . . . cheereth them in their heaviness . . .
calleth them back from their wanderings . . . raiseth them up if they
have fallen . . . counselleth them in their doubtful cases; and . . . is
a mean whereby they are fast settled in a godly course.[23]

To the objection of some, that 'they know God's Word well
enough, and therefore they need not be taught', Richard Sibbes
replies: 'The Word of God preached . . . is not altogether to teach
us, but [exists that] the Spirit going with it' might 'work grace
necessary to strengthen us in the inward man 2 Cor. 4:16. . . . Let
us therefore set a price upon God's ordinance. There must be this
dispensation.'[24] And Arthur Hildersham, in claiming that preaching 'is able to build men up in grace, as the apostle speaketh (Acts

20:32)', offers the interesting suggestion, 'therefore, though he had opportunity to write to the Thessalonians twice, yet he prayed exceedingly, as he saith (1 Thess. 3:10) that he might "see their face and might perfect that which was lacking in their faith". There is no such means to make men grow in faith and every other saving grace, to perfect that which is lacking in it, as sound preaching is'.[25]

It will be seen, therefore, that no small emphasis was placed in the Puritan writings on the vital necessity of preaching the Word of God, as distinct from merely reading it in the Bible. Indeed, John Owen is bold to assert:

> The word is like the sun in the firmament. Thereunto it is compared at large Ps. 19. It hath virtually in it all spiritual light and heat. But the preaching of the word is as the motion and beams of the sun, which actually and effectually communicate that light and heat unto all creatures, which are virtually [essentially and energetically] in the sun itself.[26]

Now it might be thought that Owen spoke a little too strongly here, but what shall we say when we find Thomas Goodwin writing deliberately:

> It is the meaning of the word which is the word indeed; it is the sense of it which is its soul . . . preaching in a more especial manner reveals God's word. When an ointment box is once opened, then it casts its savour about; and when the juice of the medicinal herb is once strained out and applied, then it heals. And so, it is the spiritual meaning of the word let into the heart which converts it and turns it to God.[27]

Certainly, where 'the atlas and axis' of Independency agree upon a thing, it is either a very knowledgeable or a very foolish man who would enter the lists against them. Perhaps, therefore, we are prepared to conclude with Nehemiah Rogers: 'The text is the word of God abridged: preaching is the word of God enlarged.'[28]

The whole subject of the good that comes to men through the preaching of the gospel, is well and thoroughly summarised by Nicholas Byfield. 'But tell us distinctly,' he makes an imaginary questioner ask, 'what good shall men get by hearing of sermons?' He answers:

> Many are the singular benefits that come to men thereby. First, the Holy Ghost is here given, Acts 10:44. Secondly, men's hearts are here opened, Acts 16:14. Thirdly, the fear of God doth here fall upon men, Acts 13:16. Fourthly, the proud and stony heart of men is here tamed, melted and made to tremble, Is. 66:2. Fifthly, the faith of God's elect is here begotten, Rom. 10:14. Sixthly, men are here sealed by the Holy Spirit of promise, Eph. 1:13. Seventhly,

here the Spirit speaketh to the churches, Eph. 1:13. Eighthly, Christ here comes to sup with men, Rev. 3:20, let men tell of their experience, whether ever their hearts tasted of the refreshing of Christ till they devoted themselves to the hearing of the Word. Ninthly, the painful distress of the afflicted conscience is here or nowhere cursed by hearing, the bones that God hath broken receive joy and gladness, Ps. 51:8. Tenthly, what shall I say, but as the Evangelical Prophet saith? If you can do nothing else, yet 'hear, and your soul shall live' Is. 55:3. Live, I say, the life of grace, yea, and the life of glory: for salvation is brought to us by hearing, Acts 28:28.[29]

A list of so many benefits which it is the special prerogative of faithful preaching to bestow, is very representative of Puritan thought on the subject, and sufficiently reveals that their elevation and defence of the pulpit was dictated, not by partiality and self-interest, but by a desire for the lasting good of the Church that then was, and the Church that was yet to be.

3. The Demands of Preaching

Preaching had its glories, but to the Puritans it also had its responsibilities – as weighty a load of them as ever mortal men were called upon to carry. 'Believe it brethren,' cried John Flavel to a meeting of fellow pastors, 'it is easier to declaim like an orator against a thousand sins of others, than it is to mortify one sin like Christians, in ourselves; to preach twenty sermons to our people, than one to our own hearts.'[30]

One who did 'preach to his own heart', throughout a life that has come down to us as a model of ministerial consistency and faithfulness, was Richard Baxter of Kidderminster. Baxter's celebrated *Reformed Pastor* is an extended sermon on the demands of the ministry. First prepared for a company of Worcestershire preachers in December 1655, in its extended form it contains many passages which stand among the most sublime and powerful prose in religious history. At the beginning of the book, Baxter considers four main areas of the preacher's life which need his constant surveillance:

1. Take heed to yourselves, lest you should be void of that saving grace of God which you offer to others, and be strangers to the effectual workings of that gospel which you preach. . . . Many a preacher is now in hell, that hath a hundred times called upon his hearers to use the utmost care and diligence to escape it. . . . Believe it brethren, God never saved any man for being a preacher, nor because he was an able preacher; but because he was a justified, sanctified man, and consequently faithful in his master's work.

Take heed therefore, to yourselves first, that you *be* that which you persuade your hearers to *be*.

2. Take heed to yourselves, lest you live in those actual sins which you preach against in others; and lest you be guilty of that which you daily condemn. . . . If sin be evil, why do you live in it? if it be not, why do you dissuade men from it?

3. Take heed also to yourselves, that you be not unfit for the great employments that you have undertaken.   He must not be himself a babe in knowledge, that will teach all those mysterious things that are to be known in order to salvation.   Oh what qualifications are necessary for that man that hath such a charge upon him as we have! How many difficulties in divinity to be opened; yet about the fundamentals that must needs be known! How many obscure texts of Scripture to be expounded. . . . It is not now and then an idle snatch or taste of studies that will serve to make a sound divine. I know that laziness hath lately learned to pretend the lowness of all our studies, and how wholly and only the Spirit must qualify and assist us to the work. . . . Oh that men should dare so sinfully by their laziness to quench the Spirit; and then pretend the Spirit for the doing of it!

4. Moreover, take heed to yourselves, lest your example contradict your doctrine, and lest you lay such stumbling-blocks before the blind, as may be the occasion of their ruin; lest you may unsay that with your lives, which you say with your tongues; and be the greatest hinderers of the success of your own labours. . . .   One proud, surly, lordly word, one needless contention, one covetous action, may cut the throat of many a sermon, and blast the fruit of all that you have been doing. . . .   We must study as hard how to live well, as how to preach well.[31]

After this, and in a succession of passages which are among the most potent even of Baxter's forceful writings, he gives eight reasons why, in answer to the demands of his preaching ministry, a pastor of souls should constantly examine his state and confirm his standing:

1. You have a heaven to win or lose yourselves. . . .   Believe it sirs, God is no respecter of persons: he saveth not men for their coats or callings; a holy calling will not save an unholy man. . . .

2. Take heed to yourselves, for you have a depraved nature, and sinful inclinations, as well as others. . . .   Alas! even in our hearts, as well as in our hearers, there is an averseness to God. . . .   Those treacherous hearts will at one time or another deceive you, if you take not heed.   Those sins that seem to lie dead, will revive: your pride and worldliness, and many a noisome vice will spring up, that you thought had been weeded out by the roots.

3. And the rather, also, take heed to yourselves, because such works as ours do put men on greater use and trial of their graces, and have greater temptations, than many other men's. . . .   It is not only the work that calls for heed but the workman also, that he may be fit for business of such weight. . . .

4. And the rather, also, take heed to yourselves, because the tempter

will make his first or sharpest onset upon you. . . . He beareth you the greatest malice, that are engaged to do him the greatest mischief . . . he knows what a rout he may make among the rest, if the leaders fall before their eyes. . . . You shall have his most subtle insinuations, and incessant solicitations, and violent assaults. As wise and learned as you are, take heed to yourselves lest he outwit you. The devil is a greater scholar than you, and a nimbler disputant . . . he will play the juggler with you undiscerned, and cheat you of your faith or innocency, and you shall not know that you have lost it; nay, he will make you believe it is multiplied or increased when it is lost. . . .

5. Take heed to yourselves also, because there are many eyes upon you, and therefore there will be many observers of your fall. You cannot miscarry but the world will ring of it. The eclipses of the sun by daytime are seldom without witnesses. . . . Take heed therefore to yourselves, and do your works as those that remember that the world looks on them, and that with the quick-sighted eye of malice, ready to make the worst of all, and to find the smallest fault where it is, and aggravate it where they find it, and divulge it, and make it advantageous to their designs; and to make faults where they cannot find them. How cautiously then should we walk before so many ill-minded observers!

6. Take heed also to yourselves; for your sins have more heinous aggravations than other men's. It is noted among King Alphonsus' sayings, That a great man cannot commit a small sin. . . . (i) You are likelier than others to sin against knowledge, because you have more than they. . . . There must needs, therefore, be the more wilfulness, by how much there is the more knowledge. If you sin, it is because you will sin. (ii) Your sins have more hypocrisy in them than other men's, by how much the more you have spoken against them. . . . O bear not that badge of the miserable Pharisees. 'They say, but do not,' Matt 23:3. . . . (iii) Moreover, your sins have more perfidiousness in them than other men's. You have engaged yourselves against them. Besides all your common engagements as Christians, you have many more as ministers. How oft have you proclaimed the evil and danger of sin, and called sinners from it. . . . Every sermon that you preached against it, every private exhortation, every confession of it in the congregation, did lay an engagement upon you to forsake it. . . .

7. Take heed to yourselves; for the honour of your Lord and Master, and of his holy truth and ways, doth more lie on you than on other men. As you may do him more service, so always more dis-service than others. The nearer men stand to God, the greater dishonour hath he by their miscarriages; and the more will they be imputed by foolish men to God himself. . . . O take heed brethren, in the name of God, of every word that you speak, every step that you tread; for you bear the ark of the Lord, you are entrusted with his honour, and dare you let it fall, and cast it in the dirt? . . .

8. Take heed to yourselves; for the souls of your hearers, and the success of your labours, do very much depend upon it. God useth

to fit men for great works before he will make them his instruments in accomplishing them. . . . If the work of the Lord be not soundly done upon your own hearts, how can you expect that he bless your labours for the effecting of it in others? . . .[32]

The demands of the preaching-office on the lives of those that bore it included strenuous day-to-day labour. Baxter gives us a most exact commentary on his own preaching, and a challenging description of what preaching should be, when he writes: 'What skill is necessary to make plain the truth, to convince the hearers; to let in the unresistible light into their consciences, and to keep it there, and drive all home; to screw the truth into their minds, and work Christ into their affections; to meet every objection that gainsays, and clearly to resolve it; to drive sinners to a stand and make them see there is no hope, but they must unavoidably be converted or condemned: and to do all this so for language and manner as beseems our work, and yet as is most suitable to the capacities of our hearers: this, and a great deal more should be done in every sermon, should surely be done with a great and holy skill. So great a God, whose message we declare, should be honoured by our delivery of it.'[33]

But this is not the work of an hour or a day; and the iron discipline of the Puritan pastors' labour through long years is well delineated, with its inevitable cost, by William Attersol:

For this, if we know not by practice, we may see by experience, that to study with constantness, to instruct with diligence, to exhort with carefulness, to reprove with zeal, to comfort with cheerfulness, to convince with boldness, to watch over people with a godly oversight, as they that must give account for their souls, to conceive godly anger and great sorrow for sin, to pray in public and private, to go in and out before the people of God in the doctrine of faith, and in example of life, to prepare themselves to handle the Word, and to deliver it with power and evidence of the Spirit, and with earnest affections; being thus prepared I say, to perform all these duties doth more consume the inward parts, waste the body, impair nature, decay strength, spend the vital spirits, and cause them to be subject to sundry infirmities, sicknesses and diseases than any [of] the strongest labour that is used among men.[34]

It is only fair to insist that as far as the Puritans were concerned, Attersol's picture of the faithful pastor was as realistic as it was idealistic, and was as truly fulfilled as it was admired. John Flavel has left us a paragraph of rare intimacy which must be quoted here, as demonstrating their real accomplishments as well as their moving spirit:

How many truths we have to study! How many wiles of Satan
and mysteries of corruption, to detect! How many cases of conscience to resolve! Yea, we must fight in defence of the truths we
preach, as well as study them to paleness, and preach them unto
faithfulness: but well-spent: head, heart, lungs and all; welcome
pained breasts, aching backs, and trembling legs; if we can all but
approve ourselves Christ's faithful servants, and hear that joyful
voice from his mouth, 'Well done, good and faithful servants'![35]

4. The Character of Preaching

It was the genius of the Puritan preaching that in style it was
plain without being dull; in emphasis, an admirable balance of
doctrine and practice; in character, faithfully devoted to the
exposition of the Word of Scripture, both letter and spirit, which
they loved.

The preaching of the Puritans was eminently plain and easily
understood. This is not to say that it was dull, far less that it was
shallow. Stories have survived of New England ploughmen
discussing for example the more abstruse points and problems of
predestination and providence, and it is well-known that the
Puritans enthused their own congregations to a great degree with
current controversies and debates, and generally educated their
people to receive the matter that they preached to them. But this
could not have been done if their preachers had preached sermons
incessantly punctuated with Latin word-plays, rounded periods and
double-barrelled words. Such preaching was considered the false
finery of the pulpit, 'court preaching'; and as the approved oratory
of the day in some circles it generally did more to increase the
reputations of the preachers than the spirituality of their hearers.
The Puritans stood in contrast to such obscure and unprofitable
rhetoric; they despised the pedantic style of a Lancelot Andrewes
or the gaudy ornaments of a Jeremy Taylor, and filled their sober,
plain teaching and exhortations with illustrations, metaphors and
similes taken from every-day life, which were easily understood and
remembered by their congregations.

Roger Ascham once remarked: 'We preachers ought to think like
great men, but speak like common people.' And in that great age
of great preachers which was the Puritan era, nothing is more
strikingly sublime than to read great and golden thinking poured
into the mould of plain and practical preaching. Nor was this a
mere political ploy to reach the ears of the growing middle-classes.

It was a matter of conviction well expressed by John Flavel that:

> a crucified style best suits the preachers of a crucified Christ. . . . Prudence will choose words that are solid, rather than florid: as a merchant will [choose] a ship by a sound bottom, and capacious hold, rather than a gilded head and stern. Words are but servants to matter. An iron key, fitted to the wards of the lock, is more useful than a golden one that will not open the door to the treasures. . . . Prudence will cast away a thousand fine words for one that is apt to penetrate the conscience and reach the heart.[36]

Richard Baxter, a master of the art of plain yet potent preaching writes in much the same vein and asks, with Baxterian logic and an air of finality: 'If you would not teach men, what do you in the pulpit? If you would, why do you not speak so as to be understood?'[37] The Puritans did preach 'so as to be understood', and to that end employed every lawful aid of native wit and acquired art; anecdote and allegory; metaphor and simile, to help gain the attention and to win the hearts and lives of their hearers for their divine Master.

If the Puritan preaching was plain, it was also thoroughly practical. The chief end of preaching, declared the Puritan brotherhood, was the glorification of God in the restoration of his image in the souls and lives of men. John Owen propounds as a principal purpose of preaching the promotion of 'the growth of light, knowledge, godliness, strictness and fruitfulness of conversation'[38] in the saints, and Thomas Manton, always representative of mainline Puritanism, observes that:

> The doers of the Word are the best hearers. That is good when we hear things that are to be done, and do things that are heard. That knowledge is best, which endeth in practice (Ps. 119:105; Matt. 7:24). . . . The hearer's life is the preachers' best commendation (2 Cor. 3:2).[39]

This desire to see their preaching result in practice is famously illustrated in the oft-quoted passage from Phillip Goodwin's *Evangelical Communicant*: 'It is reported of a good man, that coming from a public lecture, and being asked by one, whether the sermon were done, made this answer, fetching a deep sigh: "Ah! it is said, but not done." ' Certainly Puritan preachers never preached a sermon that could not be 'done'. They were masters of no divinity more than practical divinity; there was no doctrine that could not be practised, just as all good practice had to be founded on sound doctrine. They shone in doctrinal polemic, but in practical theology they blazed with warmth as well as light. They never tired of delineating the characteristics of the godly life; every twist

The above portrait of John Owen is included by courtesy of the National Portrait Gallery. John Owen is esteemed one of the great theologians of all time. To this day his reasoning is as penetrating, his biblicism as safe, his devotion as fervent, his sheer brilliance as captivating to the diligent modern mind as to our seventeenth century forebears.

and turn of the conscience that 'eschewed evil'; every labour, liberty and enjoyment of the heart that sought to walk in the ways of God; and thus they preached untiringly the practice of piety.

James Durham in his *Commentary upon Revelation* has much to say on the subject of what the Puritans called 'the application' and goes so far as to say:

> Application is the life of preaching; and there is no less study, skill, wisdom, authority and plainness necessary in the applying of a point to the conscience of hearers, and in the pressing of it home, than is required in the opening of some profound truth: and therefore ministers should study the one as well as the other. . . . Hearers are often ready to shift-by the most particular words, much more when they are more shortly and generally touched. Hence, preaching is called persuading, testifying, beseeching, entreating, or requesting, exhorting etc. All which import some such dealing in application: which is not only a more particular breaking of the matter, but a directing it to the consciences of the present hearers. And in this especially, doth the faithfulness, wisdom and dexterity of the preacher, and the power and efficacy of the gift appear.[40]

Earlier, in the same article (an appendix to his exposition of Revelation, chapters two and three) Durham lays down some rules and directions concerning this part of the preacher's work, the first of which are:

> 1. In general, we see that ministers in their application, ought to conform themselves to the case of the Church and persons to whom they preach: to erroneous people (or such as are in danger of error), more convincingly; to the secure, more sharply; to the afflicted and tender, more comfortably [encouragingly], etc. as may be seen in our Lord's dealings with these churches.
> 2. Ministers ought, in their doctrine, to apply themselves to all sorts of persons, to wit: to rulers and people; to hypocrites and openly profane; yea, to the good, and those that have most tenderness; reproving all, convincing all, as there shall be cause. . . .
> 3. This universal application to all sorts, would yet notwithstanding be managed with spiritual wisdom and prudence, so that every one may get their own allowance. Hence the Lord doth so threaten the secure and stubborn, that yet he excepteth these who were not defiled; and so comforteth the faithful, as the profane may not have a ground to take the same consolation with them. This is a main qualification of a minister of the gospel, rightly to divide the Word of Truth, and not to follow all applications promiscuously and in a heap together in any auditory, without such discriminating expressions as may guard against confusion therein: especially as to these four: (i) That a tender soul may be so strengthened and confirmed, as a secure person be not more hardened; and that a presumptuous hypocrite be so stricken at, as an exercised soul be not wounded. (ii) When both the good and profane are in one

fault, the one is otherwise to be reproved and restored than the
other; and we see Ephesus is more tenderly dealt with than Laodicea, according to the rule Gal 6:1,3.   (iii) The faults of believers
would be so reproved, as with these their state, and what is com-
mendable in their practice be not condemned and rejected also:
but that there be intermixed, commendations, or approbations of
what is approvable, lest godliness suffer when the fault of a godly
person is reproved, and lest the sentence go beyond the Master's
intent, which is not to condemn the person, but to reprove the fault.
(iv) Times and cases would be distinguished also: and where outward affliction, or inward exercise have seized on a person or people,
reproofs would be more sparing and gentle than when there is outward prosperity and a readiness to settle in a formal discharge of
duties, as by comparing the Lord's dealing with the Churches of
Ephesus, Smyrna and Philadelphia, and his dealings with Sardis and
Laodicea is clear.
4. This application would be pathetic, pungent and weighty,
according to the matter pressed, so as it may have weight upon
the conscience of the hearers.   It is a main piece of ministerial
dexterity, to make a plain, obvious, ordinary reproof, weighty in
application, so as the matter may look serious-like to the hearers, and
they be convinced that he is in earnest: and for this cause, his convictions, reproofs, directions etc., would not rest in the general, for
the Lord is particular in all these epistles: (i) In mentioning the
sins that he reproveth.   (ii) In giving the evidences of them, to
shew that he beateth not the air; and the more to bearing conviction
in the application, for as general truths will need their proofs, so
will particular applications, lest the conscience shift the challenge.
(iii) He rips up the heart, by chopping at inward sins, to wit, 'falling
from the first love'; 'thou sayest I am rich' etc.; 'thou hast a name
that thou livest, but art dead' etc. . . .   It is a main part of searching
doctrine to repel the answers that a heart may have within against
the power of godliness, though they be never expressed; and this is
a main property of the Word, to be a discerner of thought, Heb.
4. . . .[41]

From this it will be evident that Puritanism was life as well as
thought, and that the Puritan preaching aimed, not only at informing the understanding, but also at influencing the will, animating
the emotions and reforming the life.

5. *The Content of Preaching*

Of the many extracts that could be brought to bear on this point
from the Puritan writings, the following from Richard Sibbes is as
representative as it is comprehensive:

> To preach is to open the mystery of Christ, to open whatsoever is
> in Christ; to break open the box that the savour may be perceived

of all. To open Christ's natures and Person what it is; to open the offices of Christ: first, he was a prophet to teach, wherefore he came into the world; then he was a priest, offering the sacrifice of himself; and then after he had offered his sacrifice as a priest, then was king. He was more publicly and gloriously known to be a king, to rule. After he had gained a people by his priesthood and offering, then he was to be a king to govern them. . . . He was all at the same time, but I speak in regard of manifestation. Now 'to preach Christ' is to lay open all these things.

And likewise the states wherein he executed his offices. First, the state of humiliation. Christ was first abased, and then glorified. The flesh he took upon him was first sanctified and then abased, and then he made it his glorious flesh. He could not work our salvation but in a state of abasement; he could not apply it to us but in a state of exaltation and glory. To open the merits of Christ, what he hath wrought to his Father for us; to open his efficacy, as the spiritual head of his Church; what wonders he works in his children, by altering and raising of them, by fitting and preparing them for heaven: likewise to open all the promises in Christ, they are but Christ dished and parcelled out. 'All the promises in Christ are yea and amen,' 2 Cor. 1:20. They are made for Christ's sake, and performed for Christ's sake; they are all but Christ severed into so many particular gracious blessings. 'To preach Christ' is to lay open all this, which is the inheritance of God's people.

But it is not sufficient to preach Christ to lay open all this in the view of others; but in the opening of them, there must be application of them to the use of God's people, that they may see their interest [share] in them; and there must be an alluring of them, for to preach is to woo. The preachers are 'paranymphi', the friends of the bridegroom, that are to procure the marriage between Christ and his Church; therefore, they are not only to lay open the riches of the husband, Christ, but likewise to entreat for a marriage, and to use all the gifts and parts that God hath given them, to bring Christ and his Church together.

And because people are in a contrary state to Christ, 'to preach Christ' is even to begin with the law, to discover to people their estate by nature. A man can never preach the gospel that makes not way for the gospel, by showing and convincing people that they are out of Christ. Who will marry with Christ, but those that know their own beggary and misery out of Christ? That he must be had out of necessity, or else they die in debts eternally; he must be had, or else they are eternally miserable. Now when people are convinced of this, then they make out of themselves to Christ. This therefore must be done, because it is in order, that which makes way to the preaching of Christ; for 'the full stomack despiseth an honeycomb', Prov. 27:7. Who cares for balm that is not sick? Therefore we see John Baptist came before Christ, to make way for Christ, to level the mountains, to cast down whatsoever exalts itself in man. He that is to preach must discern what mountains there be between men's hearts and Christ; and he must labour to discover themselves to themselves, and lay flat all the pride of men in the dust; for 'the word of God is forcible to pull down strongholds and imaginations and to bring all into subjection to Christ', 2 Cor. 10:4. And indeed, though a man should not preach the law, yet by way of implication, all these things are wrapped in the gospel. What need of a Saviour, unless we were lost? What need of Christ to be wisdom to us, if we were not fools in ourselves? What need Christ be sanctification to us, if we were not defiled in ourselves? What need he be redemption, if we were not lost and sold in ourselves to Satan, and under his bondage? Therefore all is to make way for Christ, not only to open the mysteries of Christ, but in opening and application to let us see the necessity of Christ. In a word, being to bring Christ and the Church together, our aim must be, to persuade people to come out of their estate they are in, to come and take Christ. Whatever makes for this, that course we must use, though it be with never so much abasing of ourselves.[42]

Such a passage, by such a man, does not require the patronage of comment.

II

THE PURITAN IN THE PEW
A study in the Puritan doctrine of worship

E HAVE SEEN HOW THE PURITANS regarded the sermon as the climax of public worship; how they regarded proclamation of the Word and instruction from the Word, accompanied by the power of the Holy Spirit, as the principal mediating instrument of the power of God unto salvation and sanctification. We now turn from the practice of preaching to the practice of hearing in Puritan thought and life; from how men must preach to how they must hear the Word preached.

It has been observed that the tension between the Anglican and Puritan modes and ideals of worship arose largely from the difference between the Anglican conception of public worship as fundamentally a priestly act, and the Puritan idea of it as fundamentally a prophetic one. To the Puritan mind the priestly element in worship rested on the two great truths of Christ's perpetual High Priesthood and the consequent priesthood of all believers. Thus, any mediation of grace through the minister was not through any supposed priestly act of his, but through the Word of Christ spoken by him in the Spirit of Christ to the people of Christ. In public worship, therefore, the Puritan conceived of the prophetic element as the grand climactic and dominating factor.

This theology of the Word preached, produced a theology of the Word heard, and John Wells in his superb book *The Practical Sabbatarian*, sets the tone of his readers' approach to the ordinances of worship, and especially that of preaching, when he writes:

> Having performed . . . our morning exercises in private, how cheerfully should we repair to the public ordinances on this acceptable day of grace and salvation, when Christ sits in state, scattering

treasures of grace among the hungry and thirsty souls who are 'poor
in spirit' and waiting for spiritual alms. . . .   Public ordinances . . .
are our spiritual exchange, our holy mart, our heavenly fairs, where
we buy up, and fit ourselves with all heavenly commodities.   In
these seasons, we store ourselves with grace, knowledge and comforts
which may abundantly serve us until the revolution of another
Sabbath.[1]

Jeremiah Burroughs, in his treatise *Gospel Worship*, teaches his
readers how to 'sanctify the name of God' in hearing the Word
preached, by dividing his instruction into two parts.   Says he:
'There must first be preparation, and then an answerable behaviour
of the soul to this Word.'[2]

1. *The preparation necessary for hearing the Word preached*

'First,' cautions Burroughs, 'when you come to hear the Word, if
you would sanctify God's name, you must possess your souls with
what it is you are going to hear.   That is, what you are going to
hear is the Word of God . . . therefore you find that the apostle,
writing to the Thessalonians, gives them the reason why the Word
did them so much good as it did: it was because they did hear it as
the Word of God.   "And we also thank God constantly for this,
that when you received the word of God which you heard from us,
you accepted it not as the word of man but as what it really is, the
word of God" ' (1 Thess. 2:13).[3]

Another notable preacher, Samuel Annesley, adverting to this
point in a sermon, is aware that the limitations, both natural and
spiritual, of the preacher, known to his hearers, might obstruct
submission to the Word preached by him.   To prevent any under-
estimating of the worth of the ordinance because of this problem,
he points out that probably not even the apostles were infallibly
inspired in their ordinary sermons (or their lives, Gal. 3:11), and so
concludes:

Christ speaks through us as through a cracked trumpet, though we
betray our own frailties, yet for the main of our sermons, we dare
say 'Thus saith the Lord', which is a proof of Christ's speaking in us
(2 Cor. 13:3).[4]

If we receive the preached Word as such, Annesley assures us,
'then it will certainly "work effectually" '.

Burroughs, as his second point, continues: 'Possess your hearts
likewise with this consideration, that I come to hear the Word as
an ordinance appointed by God to convey spiritual food to my
soul.'[5]   As he says earlier, 'It is not the nature of the thing that

carries such power in it, but it is the institution of God and the
ordinance of God in it'.[6] It is the more necessary to stress this in
view of Burroughs' warnings:

> For men that are of some understanding and parts [talents], when
> they come to hear, this temptation is ready to come upon them, that
> except they hear some new thing that they did not understand before,
> wherefore should they come? . . . Now this is a great mistake.[7]

Burroughs concludes with regard to preparation for hearing the
Word of God preached:

> Pray beforehand that God would open thine eyes, and open thine
> heart, and accompany his Word; thus did David: 'Open mine eyes
> O Lord, that I may understand the wonders of thy law.' And you
> know what is said of Lydia: 'The Lord opened her heart to attend
> the Word which was spoken.' Now, seeing it is an ordinance thou
> dost expect more food from than what of its own nature [it] is able
> to convey, thou hast need to pray: 'O Lord, open mine eyes and open
> my heart: Lord, my heart is naturally locked up against thy Word,
> there are wards in my heart that, except thou art pleased to put in
> the key that may fit my heart, it will never open. . . . Lord, I have
> often gone to thy Word and the key hath stuck in it [my heart], and
> it hath not opened; but Lord, if thou wouldst but fit it and turn it
> with thine own hand, my heart would open.[8]

'Oh,' he ends, 'come with such a praying heart to the Word and
. . . God will be glorified and you will be profited.'

2. Behaviour necessary when hearing the Word preached

'First,' writes Burroughs, 'there must be a *careful attention unto the
Word*,'[9] and he explains: 'You must set your hearts unto it, as
Moses in Deut. 32:46, when he said unto the people, "Set your
hearts unto all the words which I testify among you this day, which
you shall command your children to observe to do, for it is not a
vain thing for you because it is your life".'[10] John Wells observes
on this point:

> It is said of Christ's auditors that they did hang upon his mouth
> in hearing him (Luke 19:48) . . . the ear is the proper door to the
> heart . . . study then to make it a door to salvation by a serious and
> diligent attention. . . . The ear lies in the way to the soul, as the
> light shines not into a house but by the window.[11]

Wells pleads very effectively when he adds: 'Let us not lose those
blessed truths by neglectful hearing, which Christ hath bought by
his painful bleeding.'

Samuel Annesley suggests, as an aid to all this: 'Mix your hearing

with ejaculatory prayer; ejaculations to God and soliloquies to
yourselves will help to make and keep the heart right. Jog your
own hearts as you do your sleeping neighbours. Call in your
thoughts while they are within call, and as far as possible think of
nothing but what you are about.'[12]

Burroughs gives as his second main point in the Christian's
behaviour when hearing the Word: 'As there must be attending to
the Word of God, so must there be an *opening of the heart* to receive
what God speaks to you; it is true it is a work of God to open the
heart, but God works upon men as upon rational creatures, and he
makes you to be active in opening your hearts.'[13] As John Wells
counsels: 'We must deal with our hearts to embrace the Word in the
dispensations of it. The gospel is not only to be let in by our
apprehension, but to be locked in by our affections; and we are to
entertain it, not only in the light of it, but in the love of it.'[14] He
later returns to this most vital of considerations and writes: 'The
heart is the king in the little world [of] man. . . . The inward man
must be employed in holy ordinances: not so much the ear as the
understanding; not so much the knee as the memory; not so much
the tongue as the heart, though, as our Saviour saith, Matt. 23:23,
this must be done, but the other must not be left undone.' In a
word, 'The heart is the chief guest at every ordinance.'[15]

Burroughs' third main point under this heading is made thus:
'The third thing is the careful applying of the heart to the Word,
and *an applying of the Word unto the heart*.'[16] Here, Burroughs gives a
concrete instance made the more remarkable by one of his typically
familiar and effective similes:

> Suppose thou hearest of some sin that it may be thou knowest
> thou art guilty of. Take the Word, and lay it to heart and say, 'The
> Lord hath met with my soul this day; the Lord hath spoken to me
> to the end that I may be humbled for this sin'.

Then follows his illustration:

> As a man that is asleep, if there be a noise made, it will not awake
> him so soon; but come and call him by his name, and say 'John' or
> 'Thomas', and that will awake him sooner than a great noise will;
> so, when the Word makes a noise, when it is delivered only in the
> general, men take little notice of it, but when the Word comes
> particularly to the souls of men and doth, as it were, call them by
> name, this wakes them.[17]

Another writer, George Swinnock, in the characteristically vivid
style of his *The Christian Man's Calling* has somewhat of note to say on
this point:

When the glad tidings of peace are preached, let thine heart leap with hope. Oh, let the nearer approach of the sun call forth and ripen the fruits of righteousness. When the law comes in like a corrosive, eating out the festered flesh and corruption, when the gospel is like a lenitive, both refreshing and refining thee, then they come with power; when the threatenings like wine, search the wound, and the promises, like oil, heal it, then it cometh with authority and majesty. If search be made by a reproof for thy beloved sin, do not, like Rachel, hide it, neither do thou fret when thy sore is touched, but hold thine arm forth to that knife which should prick thy vein, and let out thy bad blood. Be not angry when a prophet smites thee in the name of the Lord; believe it, he that hates thy sins most, loveth thee best. . . . Let a reproof be welcome for his sake that sendeth it.[18]

Swinnock ends his remarks on a high note of true Puritan enthusiasm: 'Oh how happy it will be for thee if whatever thine end were in going to church, yet, when thou returnest thou canst upon good ground say, "I went forth proud, but am come home humble! I went to church a bond-slave of Satan, but am returned a free-man of Christ. I went out earthly, carnal, a malicious and obstinate sinner; but, for ever blessed be the most high God, I am come back a heavenly, spiritual and gracious saint".'[19]

We turn briefly to Burroughs' fourth main point in the right behaviour of the Christian when sitting under the preaching of the Word: 'Fourthly,' he writes, 'we must *mix faith with the Word* or otherwise it will do us but little good; apply it and then believe it. In Hebrews 4:2 it is said that "The Word did not profit them, not being mixed with faith in them that heard it".'[20] Stephen Charnock, perhaps with some such text in mind, writes on this consideration, 'Without the habit [indwelling principle] of faith our persons are out of Christ; without the exercise of faith, the duties are out of Christ'.[21] Is it not sobering to be thus told that we who are in Christ can perform even worship that is outside him? As our union with Christ is glorious, our failure in worship is made the more shameful and convicting to us.

To turn once again to Jeremiah Burroughs' framework in dealing with this subject, he continues his points on how we must receive the Word as: fifthly, with meekness; sixthly, with holy fear; seventhly, with humble subjection; eighthly, with love and joy, and ninthly, with honesty.[22] This last point is taken up by John Wells in the same connection, and in speaking of it he sums up all these last points of Burroughs. Wells writes:

We are most acceptable, and most truly spiritual in ordinances, when we bring the whole man to them: when the knee doth bend, and the eye doth weep, and the heart doth yield, and the soul doth stoop and the ear incline in holy duties. God's great work was to make the whole world for man; and man's great work in spiritual approaches is to give the whole man to God. . . . If there be one wheel missing in a watch, it cannot go at all to be an index of time, and so in holy duties . . . those who serve God must give him their hottest love, their highest joy, their strongest faith, their greatest fear; they must act every grace, extend every faculty, improve every part . . . there must be head work and hand work and heart work in the ordinances.[23]

3. Duties after hearing the Word preached

Burroughs' remaining two points may be subsumed under the heading 'duties after the sermon'. His tenth direction is:

If we will sanctify God's name in the Word we must *hide the Word in our hearts*; we must not only hear it but keep it, preserve it, and then do we declare that we account the Word of God to be worth something indeed. . . . Now if I receive a thing that is of great value, if I slight it and let everybody take it from me, I do not give a testimony to the excellency of that thing; but if I take it and lock it up and keep it under lock and key I do thereby give testimony of the esteem that I have of the excellency of that thing. . . . And in Ps. 119:11, there the prophet David professed . . . 'Thy word have I hid in my heart that I might not sin against thee' . . . and then in 1 John 2:14, 'I write unto you young men because you are strong, and the Word of God abideth in you and ye have overcome the wicked one' . . . 'I have written to you young men', you that have strong natures and so strength of nature for God; but how comes this to pass? 'You are strong and the Word of God abideth in you.'[24]

Thomas Senior, in a Cripplegate sermon entitled *How we may hear the Word with profit* concludes his sermon in a most practical vein, answering the question 'But *how* shall we keep the Word'?

1. Repeat it in your families—the Bereans conned [pored] over Paul's sermons and examined his proofs and allegations: 'They received the word with all readiness of mind and searched the Scriptures daily whether those things were so.'
2. Talk of it as you go from hearing.
3. Pray to the Lord that he would preserve the word in your hearts by his Spirit—the Devil would snatch away the Word of God from us if there were not a stronger to guard it, and that is the Holy Ghost: 'That good thing which was committed to thee keep by the Holy Ghost which dwelleth in us' (2 Tim. 1:14). Pray then, after the word, as David: 'O Lord God of Abraham, Isaac and Israel our fathers, keep this for ever in the imagination of the thoughts of the hearts of thy people' (1 Chron. 29:18). And such a prayer, coming from an honest heart shall secure the word so that it shall abide

with you and it shall come after to your minds: it shall come season-
ably in the very nick and stress of exigency, and it shall come with
efficacy and power.[25]

One cannot help quoting George Swinnock at this point:

'I have read a story,' he writes, 'of two men who, walking together,
found a young tree laden with fruit. They both gathered and
satisfied themselves at present; one of them took all the remaining
fruit and carried it away with him; the other *took the tree*, and planted
it in his own ground where it prospered and brought forth fruit every
year, so that though the former had more at present, yet this had
some when he had none. Those who hear the word and have
large memories and nothing else, may carry most of the word at
present, yet, he that possibly can remember little who carries away
the tree, plants the word in his heart and obeys it in his life, shall have
fruit when the other hath none.'[26]

Finally, to return to Burroughs, he, with a true Puritan conclusion, completes his own 'particulars' thus:

11. The last that I shall speak to is this: If thou wouldst sanctify
the name of God in hearing his Word, turn it into practice, or
otherwise the name of God is blasphemed or at least taken in vain
by thee: so you have it in Jas. 1:25, 'He that is not a forgetful hearer
but a doer of the Word, this man' saith he, 'shall be blessed in his
deed'; and verse 22: 'Be ye doers of the Word and not hearers only
deceiving your own selves. . . .' So that now, put all these eleven
particulars together and then you have made good that expression
we find in Acts 13:48, that 'The Word of God was glorified'.[27]

4. A typical Puritan service

Had you entered any typical Puritan place of worship, you would
have noticed, even in the stately structures which some of them
occupied before the Ejection, a complete absence of ornament
both in the building and on the minister. The Puritan knew nothing
of sacred buildings: the 'Church' was the people in the building and
the sanctity rested in the saints, not in the place of meeting. Every
Puritan pastor would have murmured his assent to George Gillespie's
quotation from a distinguished fellow-Puritan of an earlier generation:

How much more soundly do we hold with J. Rainolds that 'Unto
us Christians no land is strange, no ground unholy; every coast is
Jewry, every house Sion; and every faithful company, yea every
faithful body a temple to serve God in'.[28]

Such an attitude enabled the Puritans after the Ejection to set up, when possible, their 'churches' in old guild-halls, warehouses, lofts and the like.

To return to the service. The sense of reverence would everywhere be felt in an atmosphere of silence broken only by the rustle of pages as the Scriptures were mulled over in the space before the service proper. The preacher entering without clerical robes or choir, a call to worship from the Bible would have begun the worship, followed by a 'prayer of approach' involving adoration, confession and supplication for blessing on the labours of the day. This might have been followed by a psalm sung either in prose or verse, often with the preacher reading out each line before it was sung for the benefit of those who could not read (this – for the preacher – unsatisfactory procedure was known as 'lining out').

There would have followed one or two readings, possibly accompanied by a brief exposition. This would have been succeeded by the sermon which generally occupied about an hour, many of the more literate taking notes, by which they would repeat the substance of the sermon to their families at home, questioning their children on some points in a catechetical way. Another lengthy prayer of intercession would have followed to be succeeded by the singing of a second psalm and the service would have ended with a benediction.

5. *Fast days*

On these occasions, normal considerations of proportion and length of service gave way to the greater part of a whole day's continuous worship, and one where prayer rather than preaching predominated. John Howe's practice on such occasions at his charge in Great Torrington, Devon has come down to us in some detail. 'He told me,' says Calamy:

> It was upon these occasions his common way to begin about nine in the morning with prayer for about a quarter of an hour in which he begged a blessing on the work of the day: and afterwards read and expounded a chapter or psalm in which he spent three-quarters of an hour. Then [he] prayed for about an hour, preached for another hour and prayed for about half an hour. After this he retired and took some little refreshment for about a quarter of an hour more (the people singing all the while) and then came again into the pulpit and prayed for another hour and gave them another sermon of about an hour's length, and so concluded the service of the day at about four of the clock in the evening with about half an hour or more in prayer.[29]

Nor was this unique or even unusual among the Puritan preachers. Philip Henry duplicated the length of Howe's fast-day service in his own church except that he did not take Howe's fifteen-minute break! His son, the famous Matthew Henry, tells us that 'he begun at nine o'clock and never stirred out of the pulpit 'till about four o'clock in the evening, spending all the time in praying, expounding, singing and preaching to the admiration of all that heard him – who were generally more on such days than usual'.[30]

It appears from this last remark that the opinion of Henry Rogers (John Howe's best biographer) that such services were 'an outrage of common sense' was not shared by the best of the Puritan congregations, several of which would attend, with their ministers, a neighbouring church's fast-services.

Perhaps the crowning glory in this field must be given to the distinguished Presbyterian Stephen Marshall and his neighbouring ministers in the metropolis. Benjamin Brook writes in *The Lives of the Puritans*:

> Mr. Marshall frequently united with his brethren in the observation of public fasts, when the services were usually protracted to a very great length. On one of these occasions, it is said, 'that Dr. Twisse having commenced the public service with a short prayer, Mr. Marshall prayed in a wonderful pathetic and prudent manner for two hours. Mr. Arrowsmith then preached an hour, then they sung a psalm after which Mr. Vines prayed nearly two hours; Mr. Palmer preached an hour and Mr. Seaman prayed nearly two hours. Mr. Henderson then spoke of the evils of the time and how they were to be remedied, and Dr. Twisse closed the service with a short prayer'.[31]

Presumably services like these, of nine or ten hours duration were not among 'the evils of the time' of which 'Mr. Henderson' spoke! As well as public and national fasts, very many fast-days were privately kept among a dozen or twenty people, in the house of a friend. Oliver Heywood, the northern Puritan, in his diaries, records his attendance at hundreds of these.

6. *The Puritan lecture*

Special mention should be made of the 'lecture' as a notable characteristic of Puritanism from its earliest days. This hallmark of Puritanism at its most powerful and potent was a sort of grandparent of our modern Bible-study: a preaching service of considerable length and great depth, usually being attended by pastors and members from neighbouring Puritan congregations. It generally took the expository form or dealt consecutively with some grand theme of Christian doctrine or practice. These lectures very often found their way into print as commentaries or treatises. Some of the series were of great length, and it became fashionable for a man to devote many years to the study of some particular part of the Scriptures as his contribution to the Church's store of divine knowledge.

Joseph Caryl, for instance, gave an astonishingly long series of 'lectures' on the book of Job which was printed volume by volume over twenty-three years to form one of the most gigantic commentaries ever written on a single book of the Bible. It occupies, in its seventeenth-century form twelve thick quartos or two colossal folios of some 2,400 pages or over 4,000 closely-printed columns: 'A vast megatherium of a book' says one writer! 'Calculated in its reading to try the virtue it chiefly inculcates,' says another. 'The author must have inherited the patience of Job to have written it and his hearers to have heard it through,' says a third. Probably few of its critics have read much of it or else they would surely have given prominence not so much to its length as to its real learning, marvellous richness or spirituality and native eloquence. Not a page could be spared, and it stands as an Everest, regal and incomparable among biblical expositions.

Nevertheless, even Caryl's feat pales somewhat in length before William Gouge's pulpit exposition of Hebrews which occupied him for no less than thirty-three years and was the substance of over one thousand sermons at his church in Blackfriars, London. Only his brief sermon-notes were published, but even they fill three large volumes in their nineteenth-century reprint! Such lectures as these also produced Jeremiah Burroughs' superb four-volume exposition of Hosea, William Greenhill's five volumes on Ezekiel, Manton on James and scores of others. Among treatises of note, Stephen Charnock's massive treatment of *The Divine Attributes* was delivered as 'lectures' as was Robert Bolton's *Instructions for a right Comforting of Afflicted Consciences* and many more.

III

THE PURITAN IN PRIVATE

THE PURITANS AS PASTORS

ROVOCATIVE AS IT MAY APPEAR, IT MUST BE
said that among the Puritans of sixteenth and seven-
teenth century England, pastoral work was not the
light and uncertain thing which it has largely become
in our own day.   Pastoral visitation was not regarded as
something conventional or socially desirable, but was
regarded as a matter of sacred and downright *business*.
For the most part, the Puritan pastor exercised his pastoral functions
in four ways, *viz*. – catechising, counselling, comforting and sharing
with his people times of special private worship.

In catechising the pastor and/or his assistant visited each household
belonging to his church in turn, examining the members of his flock
by the popular question-and-answer method on points of doctrinal
and practical divinity.   Catechisms could be learned from books
and pamphlets, or 'absorbed' from the familiar teaching of the pulpit.
Perhaps the best and most famous example of this method at work
is portrayed in the Kidderminster ministry of Richard Baxter who
crystallised the Puritan theory and practice of catechising in his book,
The Reformed Pastor.   It was always Baxter's contention that the
right use of this method lay close to the heart of the Puritan influence
wherever it was found in England.   In the preface to the book
Baxter has an illuminating example of what he felt to be the existing
need for this work:

> I am daily forced to admire how lamentably ignorant many of
> our people are, that have seemed diligent hearers of me these ten
> or twelve years, while I spoke as plainly as I was able to speak!
> Some know not that each person in the Trinity is God; nor that
> Christ is God and man; nor that he took his human nature with him
> into heaven; nor many the like necessary principles of our faith.
> Yea, some that come constantly to private meetings are grossly
> ignorant; whereas in one hour's familiar instruction of them in

private, they seem to understand more, and better entertain it, than
they did in all their lives before,

and he proceeds to outline his own method of progress in the work
of catechising which he pursued with his assistant:

> We spend Monday and Tuesday from morning to almost night in
> the work; besides a chapelry, catechised by another assistant;
> taking about fifteen or sixteen families in a week, that we may go
> through the parish, which hath above eight-hundred families, in a
> year.

Baxter recalls that he had even urged members of (the Commonwealth) Parliament to settle in each parish church a 'catechist'
particularly set apart for this work.

The counselling work of the Puritan pastor largely involved settling
the consciences of troubled Christians and of persons as yet unconverted but who were convicted of sin and seeking to know more of
the way of salvation.   With regard to the first of these: *viz.* troubled
Christians, it is interesting and significant to notice how frequent it
was for the devout Puritan to be troubled in spirit; either as to the
lawfulness of something he was doing or contemplating, or as to the
exactness of his doctrinal views.   It is a lasting feature of the
spiritually refined and well-educated soul that it is eager and urgent
not to allow any known sin to go unchallenged in life, and desires to
exalt the truth of God, even in every aspect of its religious thinking.
This sensitivity to possible error in conduct, doctrine and spiritual
standing was a mark of the Puritan congregations.   Richard
Baxter's massive *Christian Directory* is a huge folio of counsel relating
to many hundreds of questions about the Christian life, and gives a
deep insight into the Puritan pastor's ability to deal comprehensively
and deeply with such matters.

With regard to convictions of sin in the unconverted, here was a
spiritual experience deliberately fostered by the Puritan pastors and
preachers, who regarded such 'travail' as a necessary part of the new
birth and truly indicative of spiritual life begun within the heart.
One Puritan 'notable', Robert Bolton of Kettering, puts it in a book
full of these matters:

> It is the only right everlasting method to turn men from darkness
> to light, from the power of Satan unto God: and all the men of God
> and master-builders who have ever set themselves sincerely to serve
> God in their ministry and to save souls, have followed the same
> course, to wit: First, to wound by the Law, and then to heal by the
> Gospel.   We must be humbled in the sight of the Lord before he
> lift us up, Jam. 4:10.   We must be sensible of our spiritual blindness,
> captivity, poverty before we can heartily seek to be savingly en-

RICHARD BAXTER

'*While the earth remaineth*' Richard Baxter's life will provide
ministers and preachers with one of the most inspiring models of
pastoral care and forceful, clear, deep preaching. The above
picture also shows an inscription from one of Baxter's books in
the possession of the author (Richard Sargeant was Baxter's
assistant at Kidderminster).

lightened. . . . There must be sense of misery before showing of
mercy; crying "I am unclean, I am unclean" before opening the
fountain for uncleanness . . . brokenness of heart before binding up.[1]

Of his dealings with such a case, it suffices to say that the Puritan
pastor became as adept at relieving such pain of soul in the true
Christian, as he was in creating and fostering it, and it is due to
forgetfulness of the healing ministry of the Puritan preachers and
pastors that they have, in the modern mind, been so much considered all Sinai and no Calvary. For instance, Bolton himself is as
fervent and as potent in preaching the peace of the gospel as he is in
preaching the terrors of the law, and counsels the 'soundly humbled'
Christian with two great 'principles of comfort'. The one, he says,
is a principle of comfort 'from something outside' the penitent
believer, that is, the mercy of God; of which he writes:

> The mercy of God is like himself, infinite: all our sins are finite,
> both in number and nature. Now, between finite and infinite there
> is no proportion, and so no possibility of resistance. And therefore
> be thy sins never so notorious and numberless, yet (in a truly broken
> heart, thirsting for and throwing itself upon Christ, unfeignedly
> resolving upon new obedience and his glorious service for the time
> to come) [thy sins] can no more withstand or stand before God's
> mercies than a little spark the boundless and mighty ocean, thrown
> into it, nay infinitely less.[2]

Bolton's other great principle of comfort is 'something in us' *viz.* the
true desire of grace, of which he says, quoting a fellow-Puritan:

> Our desires of grace, faith and repentance, *are* the graces them-
> selves which we desire, at least in God's acceptation, who accepteth
> the will for the deed, and of our affections for the actions.[3]

To this last belongs also the *comforting work* of the Puritan pastor.
And here its most significant features were, that it was unalterably
biblical and solidly dogmatic. The Puritans were physicians of the
soul, skilled enough to avoid that vagueness and subjectiveness
which leaves the anguished mind clutching at uncertain straws with
uncertain hope. They believed the Word of God in Scripture to be
comprehensive enough to cover every basic human situation and
need, and knew their Scriptures well enough to apply, with responsible authority, the available salve to the exposed sore. They were
also clear, logical and fearless enough to set before the confused
believer his or her state in an orderly fashion, quietly and clearly
making the 'patient' understand his particular distress, what it issued
from, and where relief from it lay. People were thus turned back
from side-issues and from obsession with mere symptoms to the real
needs and proper resorts of the soul in that condition. William

Bridge's *A Lifting up for the Downcast* provides superb examples of all this; and the Puritan method throughout, will be largely seen in the ensuing matter in the present book.

Finally, the Puritan pastor's *sharing in times of special private worship* among particular families or groups of friends in his congregation formed part of his pastoral ministry. These most notably took the form of private fast-days and thanksgiving-days, and the copious diaries of, for instance, Oliver Heywood are full of records of attendances at such events. Here is an example, chosen almost at random from one of his diaries:

> Friday: we had a solemn day of fasting and prayer in my sister's house, God wonderfully assisted, there was a considerable number of people. Mr. Starkey prayed, I preached and prayed four hours. Oh, what a frame was my heart in![4]

In the following pages of this book, instead of dealing more broadly with the pastoral work of the Puritans, I have taken a 'test-case' in order to show in some detail their spiritual genius in this field. In no situation is the full genius of the Puritan pastoral theology more adequately and shiningly displayed than in their treatment of Christians suffering from *spiritual depressions* of various kinds. What was regarded as the most radical form of spiritual depression was that experience known to Puritan literature as '*desertion*' and to this we now turn.

(A) THE CONDITION OF SPIRITUAL DESERTIONS AND DEPRESSIONS

In Puritan literature on this subject, spiritual depressions, while taking many forms, were most usually caused by a lack of the sense of God's presence with the believer in love, grace and power. This period of spiritual depression (the 'dark night of the soul', the 'soul's winter-time', to use familiar Puritan phrases) was generally termed a 'desertion'. Such desertions, as we shall see, did not mean that God had truly deserted the elect soul, but the term describes the experience man-ward and as it appeared to the subject, in which the 'lively' sense of God's presence and a favourable share or 'interest' in it was denied to the Christian. Though desertion was, strictly speaking, a particular and radical form of spiritual depression, the commonness of the experience, and the complexities of the subject, often made the two terms synonymous in Puritan parlance.

That is why, in this treatment, the terms 'depression' and 'desertion' are often used interchangeably.

The first thing to be established was that a Christian may be deserted: and a Christian *as* a Christian, not as a backslidden Christian, or a secret sinner or a 'Little-Faith'. Thomas Goodwin wrote his celebrated treatise: *A Child of Light walking in Darkness* to expound its cardinal doctrine: 'That one who truly fears God, and is obedient to him, may be in a condition of darkness and have no light; and he may walk many years in that condition.'[5] Christopher Love in his, *Grace, the Truth and Growth and Different Degrees Thereof*, insists that this may happen even to a strong Christian:

> A man that hath the strength of grace, may yet want [lack] the comfort of it. Strength of grace . . . doth not exempt a man from temptations from the devil nor from desertions from God. It is an undoubted rule, there may be strength of grace where there is not the comfort and evidence of it. A child of light may walk in darkness for a time, and though he have the Holy Ghost working grace and increasing grace in his heart, yet he may want the oil of gladness, though he have received a precious anointing of grace.[6]

Joseph Symonds, in his priceless book, *The Case and Cure of a Deserted Soul*, sees this principle plainly taught in Scripture, both Old and New Testaments. It is, he writes:

> The experience of the saints . . . ask David, and you shall hear him, as soon as you come near him, sighing, sobbing, crying, roaring: but what saith he? what ails him? He telleth you, Ps. 22:1 'My God, my God, why hast thou forsaken me?' . . . But yet . . . David was here a type of Christ; and as himself was but the shadow of Christ's sorrow. David did but taste of the cup which Christ afterward drank more deeply of . . . and this cup hath gone the round ever since, so that few have ever tasted of the water of life, but they have drunk also of these waters of Marah . . . few can say they have once found God, but may say they have often lost him . . . and this I have the rather spoken that the mourners in Sion may see this uncomfortable state may consist with grace. It is a comfort to know that thy deeps are passable and thy case curable; others have walked in this heavy way and are now in heaven, others have been in these storms, yet have safely arrived at the land of promise.[7]

Many of the Puritan writers on this subject, including these already mentioned, instance the experiences of Job (chapters 13, 16, 19, 31), Asaph (Ps. 77) and Heman (Ps. 88) as further examples of Scriptural cases of desertion in the saints' experience, and convince us that, as Thomas Manton finely observes: 'Christ hath legitimated this condition and made it consistent with grace. It is a disease this, which follows the royal seed. It is more incident to the godly than

the wicked and carnal . . . those that never felt the love of Christ
. . . have none of this affliction.'[8] The same writer outlines some
of the forms these experiences of spiritual desertion take,[9] informing
his readers that there is a real desertion and an *apparent*; an internal
desertion and an *external*; a desertion as to *comfort*, and a desertion
as to grace; a desertion for *correction* and a desertion for *instruction*;
a desertion either *felt* or not felt; a total and a *partial* desertion; and
a *temporary* and an eternal desertion. Those types of desertion
italicised are those most pertinent to the subject in hand and they
will be most fully insisted upon in this treatment.

(i) *Lack of the sense of God's favourable presence*

Most prominent among the forms taken by this experience is the
lack of the sense of God's presence. As Goodwin puts it, such a
man or woman lacks 'all present sensible [felt] testimonies of God's
favour to him; he sees nothing that may give sensible present witness
of it to him . . . that light which ordinarily discovers these as
present, he is clean deprived of.'[10]

The extreme desolation to which this experience can reduce a
Christian is graphically delineated by John Wells:

> So it is with a gracious soul: wife is nothing, children nothing,
> estate nothing, friends nothing, all nothing when Christ is gone.
> What have I more, says a poor believer? And if ever poor, now he
> is so in his own apprehension. Ah, Christ is so his all, that when
> Christ is gone . . . all is gone with him: peace gone, joy gone,
> comfort gone, hope gone, faith gone, aye, and heaven gone too in
> his thoughts, and what are all his enjoyments then but dross and
> dogs-meat, but trash and lumber?[11]

(ii) *Lack of the strength of present graces*

The second form which this depression takes is weakness in the
exercise of spiritual graces and abilities. Richard Sibbes has
described the condition thus:

> They find not that former assistance in holy duties . . . they find
> that their hearts are shut up, and they cannot pray as formerly
> when they had the Spirit of God more fully; and . . . they find that
> they cannot bear afflictions with wonted patience. . . . This is first
> done when we hear the Word of God not with that delight and
> profit as we were wont. When they find how they come near to
> God in holy communion, and yet feel not that sweet taste and relish

in the ordinances of God as they were wont to do, they conclude, certainly God hath hid his face.[12]

It may be that, as William Bridge in his *A Lifting up for the Downcast* supposes, the subject of the depression becomes so discouraged that his soul 'refuses duty, and casts off duty too for present'.[13] Bridge deals graciously with such a condition, understanding that it is one of despair rather than wilfulness: 'It is possible that a good and gracious man's discouragements may extend thus far too. You will think it strange that I find an instance for this in that holy man Jeremiah; yet if you look into Jer. 20:7-9, you find it made good. . . . For the time, he did resolve to forbear preaching in the name of God, which was his duty, which he had a commission to do.'

(iii) *Unwillingness to apply present comforts*

It is Thomas Goodwin who observes:

> Those in darkness are apt to stumble at everything. So, Is. 59:10, one effect of darkness mentioned there, is to 'stumble at noonday'. So, take a soul that is left in darkness, and it will stumble at all that it hears out of the word, either in conference or at sermons; all it reads, all promises it meets with, it is more discouraged by them: 'Oh, think they, that there should be such glorious promises, and not belong to us'.[14]

'So far,' comments William Bridge on the same point, 'may the discouragements of the saints extend: Ps. 77:3, "I remembered God, and was troubled." He does not say, "I remembered my sin and was troubled," but "God"; Yea, I was not only troubled, but, "I did complain and my spirit was overwhelmed." But when the promise came, and mercy came, and comfort came, did he refuse that too? Yes, verse 2, "My soul refused to be comforted".'[15] Even the consideration of present and past graces sometimes gives the deserted soul no comfort, but his depression casts a doubt on their genuineness. Nor is this surprising, for, as Goodwin perceptively points out:

> Graces in us shine but with a borrowed light, as the stars do, with a light borrowed from the sun; so, and unless God will shine secretly, and give light to thy graces and irradiate them, thy graces will not appear to comfort thee, nor be at all a witness of God's favour to assure thee. For our spirit, that is, our graces, never witness alone; but if God's Spirit joineth not in testimony therewith, it is silent: 'The Spirit of God witnesseth with our spirits,' Rom. 8:16. Now therefore, when God hath withdrawn his testimony, then the testimony of our hearts and of our graces hath no force in it.[16]

(iv) *Lack of Assurance and fears of the future*

'To walk in darkness,' writes Goodwin, 'implies to be in doubt whither to go; so John 12:35 . . . and thus the soul of one that fears God may be filled with doubts whether God will ever be merciful to him, yea or no, and not know what God means to do with him, whether he shall go to heaven or hell . . . Ps. 77:7-9; 88:5, 6, 11, 12.'[17] Such feelings, William Bridge is sure, can even lead to a longing for death:

> Oh, says one, but I have not only cursed the day of my birth as Jeremiah, and wished I had never been born; but I am weary of life, and have sought after mine own death: and was there any godly, gracious man that was thus discouraged and cast down? Yes! What think you of Job?. . . . Thus it is with me, says Job, I am so afflicted, and distressed, and in such bitterness of soul, that I long for death, and dig for it as for hid treasures. Oh, what a mighty deep of discouragements may the saints and people of God fall into, and yet be godly and gracious.[18]

(B) THE CAUSES OF SPIRITUAL DESERTIONS AND DEPRESSIONS

Having defined and described the condition, we turn to the causes of spiritual depressions and desertions in God's people. The Puritans normally categorised these under three main heads: the Holy Spirit, our own hearts and, of course, Satan.

1 THE HOLY SPIRIT

While all desertions take place under the permissive activity of the Holy Spirit, some occur as the more direct result of God's work upon the soul, and from sovereignty in God more than sin in the subject, and out of a gracious purpose of spiritual education and advancement in the Christian. Nevertheless, Thomas Goodwin is careful to remind his readers that in attributing such experiences to the direct work of God, they must learn to distinguish between the state and some of its associated features: 'While God may be, and often is the chief efficient cause of the condition, it must be realized that he is not the author of those doubts and desperate fears and conclusions which often accompany this state. Yet, for the condition itself, it may truly be said that "the Spirit of God may concur in this darkness that befalls his child".'[19]

Further, in considering the reasons why God decrees that his people should often experience depressions and desertions of various kinds, we must ever keep in mind the major Puritan dictum: that all God's dealings with his people are in a way of grace, including his visitations of trouble. As William Bridge says in answer to the question, 'But why does God suffer his children to undergo such experiences?': 'In general, it is for their good. For their good they have peace and comfort, and for their good they lack peace and comfort.'[20] The reasons for God so dealing with his people are many, but are contained in the following seven categories in the general Puritan literature on this subject.

(i) *Out of sovereignty*

Often we must admit, as does Samuel Rutherford in his *Letters*, 'The causes of his withdrawings are unknown to us.'[21] 'One thing,' he continues, 'cannot be denied, but that ways of high sovereignty and dominion of grace are far out of the sight of angels and men.' 'Infinite sovereignty,' insists the same writer in his *Trial and Triumph of Faith*, 'may lay silence upon all hearts.'[22]

Thomas Goodwin has some perceptive observations to make upon this 'inscrutable providence' as it affected Job:

> What if God will use his absoluteness and prerogative in this his dealing with his children, and proceed therein according to no rules, case or precedent? This he may do, and, it is thought in Job's case he did . . . although the Lord had cause enough against him, yet no cause, as I remember, is pleaded . . . and therefore Elihu resolves it most of all into God's prerogative. . . . And thus also God himself, when he came to plead with Job about it, and to show him a reason of it, he only tells him how great a God he was, and therefore might do as he pleased; and useth no other arguments . . .
> God indeed never wants [lacks] a cause, nor doth deal thus where sin is not; yet, as is said of the young man, that he was blind, 'not for his sin, nor his parents' (yet not without it) 'but for the glory of God;' it was an act of God's prerogative: so here. God hath higher ends of glorifying himself in the patience, the victory and the conquest of such a champion as Job was.[23]

This is not to suppose that a person under such a desertion by sovereignty rather than by penalty has nothing within him to deserve the experience; for as sin indwells all, Joseph Symonds can rightly maintain, 'There is also a cause *in us*, though God make it not a cause to *himself* and to his action.'[24] So it was, Goodwin thinks, with Job, as we have seen. Symonds offers a maxim of much comfort to Christians in such trouble, 'If it be not for your default, it is not lost *by you*, though in such a case it be lost *to you* . . . as it is in bodily health if it depart, but not by our default . . . it is our present *affliction*, not our *fault*.'²⁵ Among his other considerations on this point, Symonds offers a basic principle of great importance: 'We are not so much to mind what God doth in the way of his free pleasure and absolute sovereignty, as what he doth in ordinary; nor so much what *he* will do, as what he will that *we* should do; nor so much what the issue of our work shall be, as what our rule is.'²⁶

Perhaps no better summary of the Puritan counselling on this matter could be given than that of Robert Asty in his book *Rejoicing in the Lord Jesus in all Cases and Conditions*:

> The Lord is pleased to act as a Sovereign in the sealing and assuring and comforting of his people. Sometimes he will come in upon a believer at his first conversion, and will fill him with joy and gladness that shall abide upon his soul many years; and sometimes the believer shall wait upon God from ordinance to ordinance, and follow him many years in the dark, and not have a discovery of his love. Sometimes the Lord will give a soul no sight of its interest [possession], nor evidence of its relation, until it come to die; and some believers have walked with the evidence of God's love in their hearts almost all their days, and when they have come to die, they have died in the dark. Sense of interest [*ie*. intuitive awareness of a share in the favour and grace of God] is under a sovereign dispensation, both as to the persons to whom it is given out, and as to time when, and as to the way and manner how.²⁷

An important second reason why the Holy Spirit often visits such experiences upon his people is:

(ii) *To show us the source of all our comforts, and our dependence upon him for them*

To quote the areas of our dependence upon God in the spiritual life, were to retail an endless list. As Joseph Symonds notes: 'Through the measure and mixture of a contrary principle: the flesh so rooted, so potent, so overspread, so active. . . . Through exigencies in our way: great fears, straits, extremities . . . through Satan's mighty and subtle temptations . . . we stand always in need of a divine presence.'²⁸ But God often withdraws the sense of such a presence that we might realise that the blessing we receive in many acts of godliness is given by God in free grace, and is not a mechanical return from the acts themselves. If it were not for these necessary, occasional 'withdrawals' of God we might swiftly begin to take from our prayers, our worship and our general obedience that assurance, satisfaction and comfort which we should seek from God alone, 'it being' as Goodwin astutely observes, 'as difficult a thing for us to go out of ourselves, and from the creatures for comfort, to God alone, as to go out of ourselves to Christ alone for righteousness.'[29]

William Bridge crystallises the point in characteristic manner, when he writes:

> So long as man has encouragement elsewhere, he does not encourage himself in the Lord his God. This being man's nature, and God having a design of love upon his own children, he permits a damp and discouragement to pass upon all their comforts: their peace to be interrupted, their hearts disquieted and their souls discouraged, so that they may encourage themselves in God alone ... God is a tender father, and he would have all the love of his children. He would not have his children to love their nurse more than himself: our joy and peace and comfort is but the nurse of our graces. Now when God sees that his children fall in love more with the nurse than with himself, then he removes the nurse, and causes their peace to be suspended and interrupted.[30]

A third, and far-reaching reason for the Holy Spirit's leading his people into and through periods of spiritual depression and desertion is:

(iii) To develop the various Christian graces in us

'There be many gracious dispositions,' Thomas Goodwin assures us, 'which actually have not opportunity to discover themselves but in case of this kind of desertion. Some of those which are the highest acts of grace and purest fruits of it, and which are the surest evidences of the truth of grace, would never appear but in case of such desertion ... would never see the light if it were not for this darkness.'[31]

(a) Faith

Above all, desertions can be used by God to strengthen that most fundamental of graces, faith. 'Learn to trust in a withdrawing God,'[32] advises Thomas Manton and it is to this degree of faith that the experience of desertion can lead us. Of this faith speaks Thomas

Brooks when he writes in his treatise, *The Mute Christian under the Smarting Rod*, 'By divine withdrawings, the soul is put upon hanging upon a naked God, a naked Christ, a naked promise, Is. 50:10.'[33] This degree of faith trusts God as he is, not as he is felt; and trusts in Christ for what he has done, not for what it has experienced of his doing. 'Then,' says Thomas Goodwin, 'faith goes wholly out of itself, as seeing nothing in itself but barely a capacity of mercy and plenteous redemption which it knows to be in God. This faith is a miracle of miracles. . . . And this is the faith . . . which we must live by when all comforts fail.'[34]

Indeed, it is this ability of faith in such circumstances which displays faith's pre-eminence among the other Christian graces, for, as Matthew Lawrence writes in his *Use and Practice of Faith*:

> When other graces and comforts to our sense lie dead and useless, even then faith lives and acts its part. It is like the cork that swims aloft, when the leads and all the net is under water.[35]

And then, in a splendid passage, this humble writer of one book concludes:

> When graces fail, performances fail, so that we abhor ourselves and duties, yet faith says, We are a holy priesthood to offer up spiritual sacrifices, acceptable to God (1 Pet. 2:5) by Jesus Christ. When Paul cried out, Rom. 7, 'Oh wretched man that I am' etc, yet by faith he can 'thank God through Jesus Christ.' When the Church is under water, yet she can speak thus in faith, Mic. 7:8, 'Rejoice not over me O mine enemy; though I fall, I shall arise again. . . .' Even when patience failed in Job, yet faith failed not.[36]

Learn therefore, urges John Flavel, to 'exercise the faith of *adherence*, when you have lost the faith of *evidence*.'[37]

(b) Humility

Desertion, claims Joseph Symonds, also 'discovers man's weakness and emptiness . . . how great the insufficiency of nature is, and how little he hath attained in grace. A child that is carried in the arms seems tall, and when it is led by the hand of the nurse and upheld, it seems to have more strength than it hath indeed; but being left unto itself, the great weakness and feebleness of it appeareth,' and so 'he shall see, that thought himself a pillar in the house of God, that he is but a bruised reed.'[38]

In his comments on 1 Peter 5:6, Robert Leighton, 'touching the matter of comfort and assurance, if it be withheld,' explains God's occasional long delays in releasing us from this condition, by observing that 'many have . . . been humbled, and yet not made humble', and insists that 'it is not enough that he hath humbled you by his hand, unless you humble yourselves under his hand.' And this goes a long way to revealing the divine beneficence in visiting Christians with such experiences, for, as Leighton assures us, 'His gracious design is to make much room for grace by much humbling.'[39]

(c) Assurance

It may seem strange that so discouraging a state should be inflicted by God for the soul's ultimate assurance; yet, the Puritan pastor assured his people, this is often the case. All God's dealings with his people are in a way of grace, and the case before us is no exception. 'God,' insists Joseph Symonds:

> gives much proof and evidence in the truth of grace which he hath wrought in them, when he makes them see they had hearts that could love him, even when it was doubtful to them whether he loved them. When the truth of grace is evidenced clearly, it brings much comfort, and what greater evidence of an upright heart, than to follow God when he seems to fly away; and to love him when he seems to abhor and hate them; to weep upon him in love when he seems armed with the weapons of death; and to pour out the soul to him, when he seems to be pouring down fire and brimstone upon them.[40]

Such a point is of great encouragement to us to continue patiently seeking the sense of God's favour again in every possible way; for when in discouragement we cease to seek, we cease to have the considerable comfort and assurance inherent in our very seeking. In a word from William Bridge, 'When God is absent from us, then we have testimonies of our love to God by our desires after him.'[41]

(d) Prayer

Thomas Goodwin tells us that sometimes God visits desertion upon his people 'to set believers' hearts a-work to pray more and more earnestly. So the apostle's buffetings, 2 Cor. 12, made him pray thrice – that is, often. . . . So Heman, by reason of his terrors, was a man much in prayers, Ps. 88:1, "I have cried day and night before thee". Christians that enjoy not communion with God, yet if they think they have not lost him, they are secure and lazy in their prayers; but if they apprehend once that their "beloved is gone" or

that they are in danger to lose him, then they will seek him all the
world over, until they will find him, Cant. 5:6-8, and make hue and
cry after him, as the Church did there.'[42]

As Robert Bolton has put it, 'That prayer is truly fervent, fullest
of spirit and enforced with most unutterable groans, which is poured
out for the recovery of God's pleased countenance after it hath been
turned away from us for a time.'[43]

(e) The fear of God

This, says Symonds, 'is not a servile fear . . . but a fear of reverence,
a fear intermixed and tempered with love,'[44] and he assures us that
often God will use spiritual depressions to breed in us that healthy,
reverential fear which should never be absent from his children:

> God will not be carelessly dealt with, though he allow us confi-
> dence and holy boldness in approach to him and converse with him,
> yet he expects a due sense of his majesty and greatness: 'let us have
> grace, whereby we may serve God with reverence and godly fear,
> for our God is a consuming fire' Heb. 12:28, 29. Though he be a
> father, yet he is a terrible, a holy and an Almighty God. . . . The
> fear of God is one of the main pillars of his throne, and so far as he
> is not our fear he is not our God: therefore he hath ever showed
> himself in his power and greatness unto men. . . . And in particular
> persons he so works by intermixtures of frowns and favours, majesty
> and mercy, that they may learn to walk as those churches did, 'In
> the fear of the Lord, and the comfort of the Holy Ghost' Acts 9:31.[45]

So much for the third main reason given for the Holy Spirit's leading
the Christian into times of spiritual depression and desertion. A
further reason in the plan of God was said to be:

(iv) *To weaken and prevent sin*

Desertion, Thomas Goodwin informs us, 'as it makes for the trial and
discovery of graces, so it is a means . . . to eat out corruptions . . . it
is a means to destroy the flesh.'[46] Joseph Symonds has much to say
in explanation of this,[47] and tells us that even when desertion is not
directly or principally a rebuke for sin, but is given for 'higher ends',
yet 'there is also a cause in us', and this, indeed, so frequently, that
'he usually doth it for sin',[48] and especially for sins treated lightly and
compromised with: 'When you are pressed to fight for Christ, and
have taken up arms against the rebels in your hearts, if you fight not

with all your strength and pursue the victory to the utmost, till you find your enemies dead before you; God may give you into their hands to lead you into captivity, and to hold you in chains that will eat into your souls, and may in your distress, stand afar off, as one that knoweth you not.'[49]

The very distress following such an experience soon puts us out of love with sin of any kind, and another writer, Christopher Love, is perceptive when he observes in his treatise, *The Dejected Soul's Cure*,

> God may withdraw his love and favour from the soul out of an act of wisdom, that thereby he may let his people see and consider that there is more evil really in sin than ever there did appear seeming good in the commission of sin . . . [and] . . . that thereby he might make his people to be more afraid of sinning against him, lest the comforts be again eclipsed; for I must reason thus, before I commit any sin, that if I do this I break the righteous law of God, and if I do break his law God will break my heart and break my peace; and shall I make no care of committing a sin against God, seeing by the committing thereof I must lie under the sense of God's wrath?[50]

Goodwin gives an eminent example from Scripture when he writes, 'The incestuous Corinthian was to be delivered to Satan – that is to be terrified – to destroy the flesh. As corrosives eat out dead flesh, so these terrors the dead corruptions; and the reviving of the guilt of old sins doth kill the seeds of those that remain in the heart'.[51]

(v) *To chastise for gross sins*

The last point brings us to a consideration that loomed large in Puritan thought upon the whole subject before us, namely, the place of gross and palpable sins as a major cause of desertions and spiritual depressions. Both Symonds and Christopher Love characterise such sins as 'the great cause'[52] of desertions, and productive of the worst depressions of all; for in such a case the believer will feel, in the quaint and memorable words of Samuel Rutherford: 'If I knew that the Beloved were only gone away for trial, and further humiliation, and not smoked out of the house with new provocations, I would forgive desertions and hold my peace. But Christ's bought absence (that I bought with my sin) is two running boils at once, one upon each side; and what side then can I lie on?'[53] Rutherford was not alone among the Puritan brotherhood

in deprecating most of all what Robert Bolton called 'the comfort-
less damp of a justly deserved desertion'.[54]

Joseph Symonds is careful to emphasise that when desertions are
for sins in particular, they are generally not for the usual 'sins of
infirmity' but for express and gross sins,[55] sins which may be clearly
detected by a prayerful enquiry, and so he writes: 'Pray the Lord
to show you wherein you have offended,'[56] and insists: 'God goeth
not away upon small offences.   You will, by searching, find the gap
that let in these floods.'[57]

The following are among those sins most frequently cited in
Puritan literature in this connection.

(a) Neglect of duties and of the exercise of graces

Christopher Love has dealt succinctly with this notable cause of
desertions, and writes:

> If we put off God without true service, God may justly put us off
> without true comfort.   This rule holds in spiritual affairs: 'He that
> will not work shall not eat.'   If we abate the sanctifying work of the
> Spirit, it is but just that God would withhold the comforting work of
> the Spirit.   The sluggard, says Solomon, hath poverty enough; so,
> if we grow lazy and sluggish in holy duties, it is just that our stock of
> comfort do decay.[58]

Here Love adds an interesting rider, when he finds a reason for
depression following such neglect, from within ourselves, as well as
from God's dealings with us: 'True grace is never so apparent to,
and sensible [felt] in the soul, as when it is in action, and therefore
want of exercise must needs cause want of comfort.'   In another
work, the same writer illustrates the intrinsically depressive qualities
of a sluggish spiritual life, when, after quoting John 14:21, he
continues:

> You know that all the stars in the firmament have light, but you
> cannot see the light of the little stars so clearly as the light of the
> greatest.   So, though there is truth of grace in the weak as well as
> in the strongest acts, yet if thy graces be weak in the exercise of them,
> thy comforts and evidences will also be weak, and hardly discerned
> and hardly seen.   'Peace be multiplied to you,' said the apostle; if
> you do not multiply your graces, God will not multiply your peace;
> if you do withdraw the exercise of your grace, God will withdraw
> the comforts of your grace.[59]

At this point, Love makes one of those rare but always pleasurable
references to a contemporary Puritan, which sums up his position:

'Grace,' saith Baxter, 'is never apparent and sensible in the soul but when it is in action; the want of action must needs cause want of assurance: though duties merit not comforts, yet they usually rise and fall with our diligence in duty.'[60] Joseph Symonds also has a great deal to say on these issues. Like so many of the Puritans, he begins by using the Song of Solomon 5:2-6, to illustrate the penal desertion of a neglectful soul, and notes the vicious circle into which such carelessness brings us:

> Sometimes the Spirit comes sweetly melting and tempering the heart to a holy softness and godly sorrow, but is quenched by negligence; therefore, justly doth the soul groan under the misery of a stupid heart, lamenting with the Church, 'Why hast thou hardened our hearts from thy fear?', Is. 63:17, and taking up that cry . . . 'I cannot repent, my heart is frozen, I cannot mourn'. . . . Sometimes he [the Spirit] cometh exciting and raising thoughts and resolutions of heart, to a more heavenly walking, but we hoist not up sails to these gales, we blow not up this spark; therefore justly are we left to a spirit of dullness, neither have life nor peace in the use of ordinances and discharge of duties.[61]

Symonds makes a further observation on this point when he reminds us that, 'Duties of godliness are not only a debt to God, but a reward to us; therefore in slightness, there is not only unfaithfulness but unthankfulness also; both the majesty and the mercy of God are despised: and can God be well pleased with such things? . . . He therefore comes with a kind of expulsion and banishment, and throweth you out of his sight, that you see what it is to dally with God'.[62]

(b) Gross sins against the light

'There is nothing in the world,' Christopher Love assures us,

> that will so much hinder him of, and keep the soul from the assurance and favour of God, as the harbouring of any known sin; for all the while David did harbour in his heart and indulge and hide his sin from God, he did lose the light of God's countenance, and he lost the shining of God's face upon his soul insomuch that he prayeth to God to restore unto him the joy of his salvation. It is true, the salvation of David was not lost, but the joy of his salvation, the comforts and consolation that he formerly enjoyed.[63]

So, he concludes, 'If you break God's law, God will break your peace'.[64] As the same writer notes in another work: 'Sin in the conscience is like Jonah in the ship, which causeth a tempest; the conscience is like a troubled sea, whose waters cannot rest: or it is

like a mote in the eye, which causeth perpetual trouble while it is
there. . . . It is just with God, that a man's own iniquities should
correct him and his backsliding should reprove him. Concealed
guilt may not bring a child of God to hell, yet for a time it may
bring a hell into his conscience.'[65]

The popular Commonwealth preacher, Obadiah Sedgwick, in his
quaintly-titled book, *The Anatomy of Sins*, forceably impresses his
readers with the seriousness of such sins in the life of the believer,
and the pain they produce. The believer, he warns:

> shall quickly find the difference 'twixt the service of God, and the service
> of sin: when he goes to pray, his sin shall meet him, and when he
> goes to hear, the ordinances shall cast his sin into his face. As
> Samson, when he lost his hair, he could not do as formerly, as at
> other times; so, even actual dominion of sin, though it doth not
> nullify the relations, yet it wonderfully varies the condition: the sun
> seems to be darkened at noonday, the air is filled with tempest and
> thunders which lately was overspread with beautiful light; God
> looks in terror and displeasure, and the conscience wounds with
> closest bitterness. All former comforts seem to take leave of us.
> Sometimes we are so distressed, that we fear we are lost for ever.
> One such sinning may cost us many years of cruel vexation; and of
> this we may be sure, that till we are soundly humbled and renew
> our repentance, we shall never see a smile in God's countenance, nor
> hear a good word from conscience.[66]

(c) Sins of long ago

'It is possible,' Joseph Caryl maintains in his massive exposition of
Job, 'that even they who have truly repented of the sins of youth,
may yet feel the grief of them in old age: for though such shall not
be punished for the sins of youth, yet they are often chastened for
them; and though God will not remember their sins against them,
yet he may give them such mindings of them as to make their hearts
to ache and themselves to cry out.'[67] Sometimes, of course, 'a
godly man may remember his old sins with new fears' owing to the
work of Satan, one of whose devices, Caryl warns us, is 'to fill them
with assurance of pardon who are under guilt', and conversely, 'to
fill those with doubtings that they are not pardoned who are acquit-
ted from guilt'.

Nevertheless, the same writer insists, 'God himself may, for a time,
or for our trial, make us possess the guilt of it, and leave us to the
questionings of past pardon'.[68] That God has a good and wise
purpose in this, is made clear by Robert Bolton, who expounds the

Courtesy of the British Museum, Lon[d]

RICHARD SIBBES

Stateliest of figures in Puritanism, Richard Sibbes' influence pervaded every part of the Puritan movement in his day—from the humblest ploughman reading his 'Bruised Reed' to the nobleman and the scholar deep in his splendid 'Expositions' of Paul.

Vera Effigies
THOMÆ GOODWIN: S.T.P.
Obijt Ætatis 80. 1679.

For a generation to produce only one really great theologian in
the Church's history is admirable. Yet the same generation that
produced an Owen gave us also a Goodwin, who, with his
majestic grasp of theology linked to a warm and visionary delight
in the wonders of grace, stands as one of the greatest
'experimental' theologians we have ever had.

point in some detail in an arresting passage in his earlier cited, *Instruction for a Right Comforting of Afflicted Consciences*:

> Sometimes, the Lord may for a time retire the light of his countenance . . . from his child, that he may be driven thereby to take a new and more exact revision, a most serious, thorough survey of his youthful sins, of that dark and damned time which he wholly spent upon the devil; and so [be] put again, as it were, into the pangs of his new birth, that Christ may be more perfectly formed in him: that he may . . . renewing his sorrow, and repairing repentance, grow into a further detestation of them, a more absolute divorce from his insinuating minion-delight, and be happily frighted afresh and fired for ever from the very 'garment spotted by the flesh' and all appearance of evil.[69]

Especially, Bolton claims, God may visit such desertions upon his people in grace,

> if penitent grief and trouble of conscience . . . were not in some good measure answerable to their former abominable life and sinful provocations; if they have been extraordinary sinners and but ordinary sorrowers for sin; if they were formerly furious in the service of Satan, and now but something faint-hearted in standing on God's side; if heretofore they marched impetuously like Jehu in the pursuit of earthly pleasures, and now creep but slowly forward in the ways of God. . . . In such cases, the Lord may withdraw himself in displeasure, leave them for a time to the terrors of their own hearts, all their old sins may return to the eye of their consciences as unremitted . . . that so their regeneration may be, as it were, regenerated; their new birth new-born, their sins . . . more hated and abhorred.[70]

'In such a case,' concludes Joseph Caryl, 'the sins which have been pardoned, are pardoned again: not that the first pardon is recalled, but cleared, and faith strengthened that we are pardoned.'[71]

(d) False confidence and pride

Nehemiah Rogers characterises this type of sin as 'a dangerous sin, and such a sin as the best of God's children are prone unto: a disease that the very elect are sick of'.[72] Thomas Goodwin has some characteristically acute observations to make at this point. Suggesting that David, in Psalm 30, is a noteworthy example of a believer deserted because of false confidence in himself (vs. 6,7), Goodwin notes that such carnal confidence is produced, 'when we trust to false signs shuffled in among the true',[73] when believers, having sound evidences of a good standing before God, 'do often rake together many other signs that are but probable, yea, and which are deceitful and but common to hypocrites'. Desertion in such cases, it is maintained, will win us back from such false grounds of confidence: 'Now God, to discover which are false, and which are not, leaves a man; and then he will find all his false signs to leave him, as flatterers use to do, and to be but as broken teeth among those which are sound and whole.'

False confidence is also often engendered and desertion invited, says Goodwin, 'when we put too much of our confidence upon signs, though true, and trust too much to our comforts and former revelations, and witnesses of God's Spirit, and to our graces, which are all but creatures [created things], acts of God upon us and in us. When, therefore, we let the weight of our support to hang on these, God, in this case, often leaves us, "that no flesh should glory in his presence" '.[74]

William Bridge has written with great effect on this very matter:

> When a man draws his comfort only from something that he finds within himself; from grace that he finds within, and not from grace without; from Christ within, and not from Christ without, then his comfort will not hold. . . . Grace without is perpetual, that is to say, Christ's own personal obedience, in the merit of it, is perpetual. But the actings of grace within us are not perpetual, or not perpetually obvious to sight, and therefore cannot perpetually comfort. . . . When therefore, you see the streams of a man's comfort run in this channel, when he draws all his comfort only or principally from . . . the actings of grace within, then you may say: Though the stream be now full, stay but a little, and ere long you will see it dried, and this man will be much discouraged.[75]

(e) Grieving the Holy Spirit

The Puritan theologians generally rejected the idea of passions being resident in the God-head, and were careful to explain anthropomorphic statements and descriptions about God in Scripture as relating to their effect in the object (man) rather than to their proper existence in the subject (God).

For instance, with regard to the 'grieving' of the Holy Spirit, both Sibbes and Owen are quick to interpret the phrase as, in Owen's words, the doing of 'those things that are proper to grieve him, though he be not passively grieved; our sins being no less therein than if he were grieved as we are',[76] and, as Sibbes puts it, 'when we do that whereupon the Spirit doth that which grieved persons so; that is, retireth and sheweth dislike, and returns grief again'.[77] Both Sibbes and Owen agree that this is a necessary reduction of the common import of the term 'grief', for, as Sibbes asserts, 'The Holy Ghost cannot properly be grieved in his own person, because grief implies a defect of happiness, in suffering that we wish to be removed'.[78] Owen puts it thus: 'The Spirit cannot be grieved, or affected with sorrows; which infers alteration, disappointment, weakness – all incompatible with his infinite perfections.'[79]

Yet these same writers, and all the Puritans whom they represent, realise that anthropomorphisms in Scripture, while metaphorical by definition, yet denote somewhat in the Deity answerable to human feelings, and identifiable in such terms. 'These affections,' writes Owen elsewhere,[80] 'doth God take upon himself for our instruction;' they denote 'great and signal actions' of God 'which could proceed from no principle that we can apprehend but great trouble and molestation' in him. As Sibbes puts it: 'Though the passion of grief be not in the Holy Ghost, yet there is, in his holy nature, a pure displeasure and hatred of sin, with such a degree of abomination as, though it tend not to the destruction in the offender, yet to sharp correction; so that grief is eminently in the hatred of God in such a manner as becomes him.'[81]

While many sins are mentioned in the Puritan writings as causing this 'grieving of the Spirit', it is especially the attitude of the heart in the sin, rather than the sin itself simply considered, which makes it a sin grieving to the Holy Ghost (Ps. 95:10).

Where the Christian is not overcome by the sudden violence of temptation, but the sin grows out of the disposition, in neglect of good or commission of evil, it is then that, in the words of Joseph Symonds, 'we grieve the Spirit, and so procure the effects of offence and grievance [viz.], God's withdrawing from us, and leaving us to the unhappy state of a withering and languishing spirit'.[82] It is at such times that the soul feels the force of Christopher Love's words: 'If you grieve the Spirit of God, it is just with God to grieve your spirits: you never send God's Spirit sad to heaven, but God may make sad your spirits on earth.'[83]

Such were, to the Puritan pastor, some of the most common sins against light which brought the Christian into periods of depression and desertion under the chastening and corrective work of the Holy Spirit.

A further main reason following upon those given previously, why God visits such experiences upon his people, is:

(vi) To keep believers near to himself

'God forsakes us,' declares Matthew Lawrence, 'that we may not forsake God,'[84] and Thomas Brooks familiarly expounds the sage but cryptic remark:

> By God's withdrawing from his people, he prevents his people's withdrawing from him; and so by an affliction he prevents a sin. For God to withdraw from me is but my affliction, but for me to withdraw from God, that is my sin, Heb. 10:38-39; and therefore it were better for me that God should withdraw a thousand times from me, than that I should once withdraw from God. God therefore forsakes us, that we may not forsake our God.[85]

Joseph Symonds, as we have come to expect, puts the issue memorably when he writes, 'And this advantage comes by desertions: that the soul is so frightened with those storms which it met with, that it is afraid to be any more out of its harbour, but seeks to dwell under the wing of Christ, and to keep closer to him than ever it did before'.[86] The result of such benevolent desertion is, as Robert Bolton points out, that, 'the privation of excellent things hath special power to raise our imaginations to an higher strain of estimation of them; and to cause us, as their return, to entertain them with much more longing, far dearer apprehensions and embracement'.[87] William Bridge reduces the whole operation to the principle that, 'the interruption of an ordinary blessing does raise it to an extraordinary',[88] and illustrates this delightfully:

> So long as a man has his health and strength, though he be able to travel forty, fifty, three-score miles a day, he is not much affected therewith; but if he be sick a little, and at death's door, and then begins to recover, though he can but put forth his hand, or stir his leg, he blesses God, and says, 'Oh, dear friends, I can stir myself in my bed, I can move my hand or my leg; what an extraordinary mercy and blessing this is!' So in this case, so long as a man has his inward peace and quietness of soul without interruption, he looks upon it as a common mercy and blessing; but if his peace be a little interrupted, and his soul buffeted by Satan, and then he recovers his peace, 'Oh'! says he, 'what an extraordinary blessing and mercy is this!' Now God will sometimes raise the price of this commodity from an ordinary to an extraordinary blessing, and therefore he doth permit his own children and dearest servants to be thus discouraged, and their peace interrupted.[89]

The last reason which will be given here for God more directly leading his people into these experiences is:

(vii) That believers may help others from their own experience

A prominent reason given for desertions and spiritual depressions in the Puritan writings, was that the Christian who had passed through such experiences, was able, more effectively than most, to comfort those undergoing the same experience. Thomas Goodwin has written feelingly and with care on this point, speaking of the time when God 'intends to make a man a wise, able, skilful and a strong Christian; wise, namely in this, which is the greatest learning and wisdom in the world, to comfort others'.[90]

> This may seem to be the reason of his dealing with Heman. Heman was brought up in this school of temptation, and kept in this form from a youth, Ps. 88:15. . . . Yet, in the end, when God raised him up again, this Heman, who lived about David and Solomon's time, is reckoned among the wisest of his time, of one of the four that were next to Solomon for wisdom, 1 Kgs. 4:31. So, that great apostle was a man exposed to the same combats that others were; he was buffeted by Satan, 2 Cor. 12, filled with inward terrors as well as those without. What was this for? Not so much for any personal cause of his own, as to make him able to comfort others, 2 Cor. 1:4,5. For that comfort which answereth a temptation in one man's heart, will answer the same in another's. When temptations have the same wards, that key which unlocked one man's bolts will serve and answer to another's. . . . This act of speaking peace and words of comfort in season, is the greatest wisdom in the world, and is not learned but in Heman's school.[91]

Nathaniel Whiting has much to say of value here. An obscure Puritan pastor, he published only one book as his contribution to the sacred literature of the day, quaintly entitled, *Old Jacob's Altar Newly Repaired*, the unusual thesis of which is that it is the duty of God's people to record and relate their experiences of 'dangers, deliverances and duties' to each other's comfort and edification. On the point now before us, he writes:

> I am much persuaded that if an experienced Christian would make a humble and faithful narrative of his own condition to a deserted saint, and tell him, 'Such has been my case: time was when the Lord hid his face from me, when the loving kindnesses of God were shut up in displeasure against me, when I had lost all communion with God, all sense of pardoning and accepting grace with God, when I could not pour forth my soul in prayer unto God, and when I had no incomes by way of comfort from God . . . but by the goodness of the Lord, the mist is broke up, the clouds are scattered, the face of God appears again, and I find joy and peace and comfort in my soul: yea, the beams of God's favour shine brighter, and the streams of consolation run on more fresh and freely than ever they did . . .' Is. 54:7-9. Oh sure these experiments as to desertion and

as to consolation . . . would marvellously revive a drooping saint, and make his stooping heart glad. My reasons are these:

1. Because the methods of God in correcting and comforting his people are the same, their trials and their triumphs are alike; as 'face answers face in a glass', so the condition of one saint answers another. . . .

2. Because these experiments gain much authority with us . . . 1 John 1:3.

3. Because God will hereby set a greater mark of honour upon the saints, and make them with more affectionateness love one another when they find that eye hath need of hand, and the head of the foot, 1 Cor. 12:21, that they are mutually dependent upon and mutually serviceable one to another.[92]

That such a ministry of comfort is specialised, and the more valuable for its rarity is a point well made by Christopher Love: 'A scholar may read much of the sufferings . . . that other Christians have lain under . . . but yet, for all that reading, he may not be so able to pity distressed souls because he wanteth experience of it himself. A scholar may read books on the art of navigation, and yet he may not be a good mariner, but it is experience that makes them to be good mariners . . . those that have been tempted, those whose consciences have been troubled, those are the fittest men to succour those that are in that condition; God chooses broken vessels to pour comfort into, that they may diffuse it unto others.'[93]

2 OUR OWN HEARTS

Writes Thomas Goodwin: 'That our own hearts should be causes and producers of such distress and darkness when the Holy Ghost thus deals with us, is no wonder, because as we are creatures, there is much weakness and infirmity in us . . . by reason of which, if God doth but hide himself and withdraw his presence which supporteth us in comfort as in being, we are ready presently to fall into those fears of ourselves. . . .   And no less, but far greater is the dependence of the new creature upon God's face and presence that it cannot be alone and bear up itself, but it fails if God hide himself . . . as children left alone in the dark are afraid of bugbears and they know not what, and are apt to stumble and fall, which is by reason of their weakness; so it is with the new creature in its childhood here in this life. "It was my infirmity" says David, and again "Thou didst hide thy face and I was troubled" Ps. 30:7.'[94]

The 'bugbears' of the heart in spiritual darkness are many, and generally occur as the result of human judgments and emotions unregulated by the Word and the Spirit of God. These problems, some of which have received much attention in our own day, but which were not at all unknown to the Puritan pastors were:

(i) Mental Depression

This was known in the language of Puritan England as 'melancholy' and was usually defined as that condition of mental depression for which the subject could offer no coherent reason, and which was produced by natural, psychological or bodily (as distinct from truly spiritual) causes. Christopher Love briefly but comprehensively summarises the symptoms and effects when he says that because of it: 'The understanding may be darkened, the fancy troubled, reason perverted and the soul saddened.'[95] Of it Thomas Brooks writes, in his usual graphic style:

> Melancholy is a dark and dusky humour which disturbs both the soul and the body, and the cure of it belongs to the physician [rather] than to the divine. . . . It is a humour that unfits a man for all sorts of services, but especially those that concern his soul, his spiritual estate, his everlasting condition. The melancholic person tries the physician, grieves the minister, wounds relations and makes sport for the Devil. . . . Melancholy is a disease that works strange passions, strange imaginations and strange conclusions.[96]

Elsewhere he illustrates this last sentence: 'Look, as coloured glass makes the very beams of the sun seem to be all of the same colour with itself – if the glass be blue, the beams of the sun seem to be blue . . . so this black, melancholy humour represents all things to the eye of the soul as duskish and dark, and as full of horror and terror. Yea, many times it represents the bright beams of divine love and the shinings of the Sun of Righteousness, and the gracious whisperings of the blessed Spirit as delusions and as slights of Satan to cozen the soul.'[97]

Richard Baxter has written copiously upon this matter both as a pastor and a 'lay physician', and much of his teaching is summarised in a Cripplegate sermon of great length entitled, *The Cure of Melancholy and Overmuch Sorrow by Faith and Physic*. Speaking of the effect of such mental depressions on the Christian and his spiritual life, Baxter observes:

> The passions of grief and trouble do oft overthrow the sober and sound use of reason; so that a man's judgement is corrupted and perverted by it, and is not, in that case, to be trusted: as a man in raging anger, so one in fear and great trouble of mind thinks not of

things as they are but as his passion represents them. About God and religion, and about his own soul and his actions, or about his friends or enemies his judgement is perverted and is usually false."

Such a condition, he assures his hearers, is of such dominating force that: 'You may almost as easily keep the leaves of trees in quietness and order in a blustering wind as the thoughts of one in troubling passions.'" Yet it is to such a condition, with all its complexities, that he addresses himself in the sermon. And here, after speaking more than once of the principal difficulty of convincing such a depressed Christian that his trouble is constitutional and natural, not spiritual, Baxter goes on to give some helpful practical counsel:

> Perceive that your understandings are not now so sound and strong as other men's . . . believe wiser men and be ruled by them . . . ask the minister or friend what he thinketh of your condition and believe him and be ruled by him rather than by your crazed self.
>
> Do you find that your troubles do you more good or hurt? . . . and will you cherish or plead for the work of Satan which you find is against yourselves and God?
>
> Avoid your musings, and exercise not your thoughts now too deeply nor too much. Long meditation is a duty to some but not to you—no more than it is a man's duty to go to church that hath his leg broken or his foot out of joint: he must rest and ease it till it be set again and strengthened.
>
> You must not be much alone. . . . Nor must you be long in secret prayer but more in public prayer with others.
>
> Let those thoughts which you have be laid out on the most excellent things. Pour not all on yourselves and on your distempered hearts: the best may find *there* much matter of trouble! . . . If you have any power of your own thoughts, force them to think most of these four things: . . . the infinite goodness of God, who is fuller of love than the sun is of light . . . the immeasurable love of Christ in man's redemption and of the sufficiency of his sacrifice and merits . . . the free covenant and offer of grace . . . the inconceivable glory and joy which all the blessed have with Christ, and which God hath promised with his oath and seal to all that consent to the covenant of grace and are willing to be saved and ruled by Christ.
>
> Use not yourselves to a complaining talk, but talk most of the great mercies of God which you have received.
>
> Especially when you pray, resolve to spend most of your time in thanksgiving and praising God. If you cannot do it with the joy that you should, yet do it as you can.
>
> When vexations or blasphemous thoughts are thrust into your minds by Satan, neither give them entertainment nor yet be overmuch troubled at them.
>
> Again, still remember what a comfortable evidence you carry about with you that your sin is not damning while you feel that you love it not but hate it and are weary of it. Scarce any sort of sinners

have so little pleasure in their sin as the melancholy, or so little desire to keep them, and only beloved sins undo men.[100]

In all this there is evidence enough of some sound psychology in the Puritan approach to mental depressions, especially in their real awareness of the distinction between mental and spiritual depression. It is not only amusing that Baxter includes into the written sermon quoted above several pages of medical 'remedies' and an amazing medley of antique potions and treatments: it also shows an awareness that, as Thomas Brooks puts it in a footnote, 'The cure of melancholy belongs rather to the physician than to the divine, to Galen than to Paul',[101] and that the foregoing counsel relates not so much to the condition as to the Christian in the condition.

The next two factors contributing to spiritual depressions that shall be noted are dealt with briefly here, as they re-appear in more detailed consideration under the section dealing with Satan's part in provoking spiritual depressions and desertions.

(ii) False Reasonings unregulated by Scripture

Thomas Goodwin has written acutely on this point to show that human reason not regulated and governed by the Word of God is an inadequate and dangerous guide in spiritual matters after, as well as before conversion, and can often cause spiritual depressions and a sense of spiritual desertion.

> As men that want [lack] true faith, the unsound hearers of the Word . . . are . . . apt through carnal reason misapplying the word they hear, to frame and draw from thence . . . multitudes of false reasons to uphold and maintain to themselves a good opinion of their estates: so, on the contrary, in those who have true faith, all that carnal reason which remains in great measure unsubdued in them is apt to raise and forge as strong objections against the work of faith begun, and as peremptorily to conclude against their present estate by the like misapplications of the word, but especially by misrepresenting God's dealings towards them. And they, being sometimes led by sense and reason whilst they walk in darkness, they are apt to misinterpret God's mind towards them rather by his works and dispensations which they see and feel, than by his Word which they are to believe.[102]

Goodwin quotes Gideon in Judges 6:12,13 and Asaph in Psalm 73 as examples of this failing, and while he does not derogate from human reason in its right place, he insists that it is subordinate to the higher reason which speaks in revelation. Where it is preferred before the mind of God, reason usurps supremacy over man, and this very situation, insists Goodwin, is most commonly achieved in times of trouble or spiritual desertion which, as a result, can easily develop into the more sinister state of mental depression:

> And to conclude this: if in any condition that befalls God's child carnal reason hath the advantage and upper ground of faith, it is now . . . when it walks in darkness and hath no light . . . when faith is under so great an eclipse.[103]

(iii) *Human Emotions unregulated by Scripture*

Unsanctified reason in the Christian doubles back on its tracks as it were, and now questions the believer's true standing in grace, whereas before his conversion it complimented him on his false self-righteousness. In a similar way, unsanctified emotions in the Christian often betray him into unfounded fears, where before they betrayed him into groundless presumption. Goodwin lists five reasons why the believer is susceptible to such new extremes of doubt and even despair in times of desertion:

> 1. Because that in the work of humiliation which prepares for faith . . . a man is for ever put out of conceit with himself as of himself. At which time also –
> 2. He was so thoroughly and feelingly convinced of the heinousness of sin which before he had slighted, that he is apt now . . . to be jealous of God lest he might have been so provoked as never to pardon him. And –
> 3. Having through the same conviction the infinite terror and deceitfulness of his heart before (in flattering him and judging his estate good when it was most accursed) so clearly discovered and discerned, he thereby becomes exceeding jealous and afraid of erring on that hand still, and so is apt to lend an ear to any doubt and scruple that is suggested. Especially –
> 4. He being withal made apprehensive . . . of that infinite danger to his eternal salvation there may be in nourishing a false opinion of the goodness of his estate . . . so he thinks it safer to err on that hand than the other. And –
> 5. Being also sensible of what transcendent concernment his eternal salvation is of (which before he slighted), this arouseth suspicion which in all matters of great consequence and moment is always doubting and inquisitive.[104]

The wisdom of such emphatic teaching is soon seen clearly when the depressed and discouraged soul learns the deceitfulness of the heart in condemning as well as in flattering, and determines to trust in nothing but God and his Word.

3 SATAN

After God himself and the believer, a third major cause of spiritual depressions and desertions was found in the activity of Satan.

(i) That he does it

To the Puritan mind Satan was never far from the saints, and the devil loomed as large in their writings and sermons as he did in the consciousness of those for whom they wrote and preached. Consequently, Satan's part in spiritual depressions received sharp attention from the Puritan pastors. As a creature of limited power, his power to depress and discourage Christians was not considered absolute but contingent: contingent not only upon God's permission, but also upon our weakness and sinfulness, as well as our foolish receiving of his suggestions. Thomas Goodwin observes:

> As God says of those enemies of his church, Zech. 1:15, 'I was but a little displeased, and they helped forward the affliction', so when God is angry with his child, and but a little, and doth hide his face but for a moment, yet Satan watcheth that hour of darkness, as Christ calls it, Luke 22:53, and joins his power of darkness to this our natural darkness, to cause, if possible, blackness of darkness, even utter despair in us.[105]

Goodwin is sure that, 'unless he had furtherance from beneath, even from those principles of guilt and darkness in us before mentioned, he could not disquiet us'.[106] Richard Sibbes puts it vividly enough in *The Soul's Conflict*: 'It is Satan's practice to go over the hedge where it is lowest.'[107]

That Satan increases depressions and the pain of desertions where he may, is clear, not only from experience, but also from a consideration of his very nature as 'tempter', the 'adversary' and 'accuser of the brethren', and his native malice. 'It is,' says Sibbes, 'his continual trade and course to seek his rest in our disquiet; he is by beaten practice and profession a tempter in this kind.'[108] Sibbes traces this activity of Satan to his standing motive when he writes: 'By his envy and subtlety, we were driven out of paradise at the first, and now he envies us the paradise of a good conscience. When Satan seeth a man strongly and comfortably walk with God, he cannot endure that a creature of meaner rank by creation than himself should enjoy such happiness.'[109]

The result of this envy is shown by Christopher Love: 'When he cannot do the greater,' he 'will do the less: and if he cannot damn

thy soul, he will labour all he can to disquiet thy conscience.   The
devil aims principally to make us walk sinfully, and if not, then
uncomfortably.'[110]   The same writer, in another work, expounds this
more clearly:

> Because he cannot make the children of God to dash their souls
> in pieces upon the rocks of presumption, therefore he labours to
> make them to drown their souls in the gulf of desperation; because
> he cannot hinder a child of God from going into his master's joy in
> another world, he labours to hinder their master's joy from coming
> into them in this world.   The devil will rather play at small game
> than at no game at all: seeing he cannot keep them from going into
> heaven itself, he will keep heaven from entering into them; because
> he cannot keep you from the having of grace, he will keep you as
> long as he can from having the sense of grace.[111]

(ii) Why he does it

Richard Gilpin has a notable treatise, *Demonologia Sacra, or a
Treatise of Satan's Temptations*, in which he has a great deal to say of
Satan's part in fostering spiritual depressions.   Among the several
reasons why Satan does this, Gilpin adduces two main ones.   First,
Satanically-increased depressions 'do take away all alacrity and
forwardness of the mind partly by diverting it from duty.   Sorrows,
when they prevail, do so fix the mind upon the present trouble, that
it can think of nothing but its burden',[112] with the result that, 'As
the mind (in trouble) is wholly employed in a contemplation of its
misery, rather than in finding out a way to avoid it; so, if it be at
leisure at any time to entertain thoughts of using means for recovery,
yet 'tis so tired out with its burden, so disheartened by its own
fears, so discouraged with opposition and disappointment, that it
hath no list to undertake anything'.[113]   If the person does break
through such fatal lethargy, Gilpin exposes a further stratagem of
Satan: 'Troubled spirits have commonly great expectations from
duties at first, and they run to them (as the impotent and sick people
to the pool at Bethesda) with thoughts of immediate ease . . . but
when they have tried, and waited a while . . . and yet there is no
voice nor hearing, no answers from God, no peace . . . 'tis easy for
the Devil to add, "And why do you wait on the Lord any longer"?'[114]
This resort, Gilpin informs his readers, is generally followed up with
a whole variety of inducements to lead the soul to the abandonment
of religion altogether.   One more reason of note which Gilpin gives

as to why Satan involves himself thus in the desertions of the saints,
is that:

> Satan makes use of the troubles of God's children as a stumbling-
> block to others. 'Tis no small advantage to him, that he hath
> hereby an occasion to render the ways of God unlovely to those that
> are beginning to look heaven-ward; he sets before them the sighs,
> groans, complaints and restless outcries of the wounded in spirit, to
> fear them off from all seriousness in religion, and whispers this to
> them: 'Will you choose a life of bitterness and sorrow? Can you eat
> ashes for bread, and mingle your drink with tears? Will you
> exchange the comforts and contents of life, for a melancholy heart
> and a dejected countenance? . . .' Thus he follows many young
> beginners with his suggestions, making them believe that they cannot
> be serious in religion but at last they will be brought to this, and that
> it is a very dangerous thing to be religious over-much, and on the
> highway to despair: so that if they must have a religion, he readily
> directs them to use no more of it than may consist with the pressures
> of sin and the world, and to make an easy business of it.[115]

(iii) How he does it

Much could be said of Satan's motives, but it is of greater consequence now to examine the methods he uses to cast a Christian
into further depths of spiritual depression. We come, then, to a
topic which many of the Puritans regarded as one of the most
complex in practical divinity viz. unraveling and answering the
strategems by which the Devil seeks to cast the soul into despair.
We will mention four main areas of assault, any one of which is dealt
with in great detail in treatises of the period.

(a) Using carnal reasonings

By the suggestion and encouragement of false reasoning, Satan
brings many of God's people to the edge of despair. His astuteness
here, in the region of the thoughts and reasonings of the mind, is
briefly but forceably characterised by Thomas Goodwin when he
reminds us, 'A student he is of five thousand years standing, that
hath lost no time, but as he is said to "accuse day and night" (Rev.
12:10), so is able to study both day and night; and he hath made it
his chief, if not his whole study, to enable himself to tempt and plead
against us. It is his trade'.[116] Pre-eminently, of course, Satan's
design in intruding or inciting false reasoning in depressions, is to

convince the soul that it is unsaved and even reprobate. 'The objections and difficulties which the believer meets with in beating out a right judgment of his estate,' insists Goodwin,

> are greater than in any controversy the world ever knew, and afford stranger knots, and require as acute distinctions to dissolve them; and indeed such as did not the Holy Ghost sometimes cut, but sometimes untie them for believers by witnessing with our spirits that we are the sons of God, bare reason alone could never determine in it. Now Satan, through long experience and observation, hath all these at his fingers' ends, and hath reduced them all to commonplaces long since. He hath still observed and laid up what answers have relieved the spirits of believers in such and such a doubt cast in by him, and then studies a further reply against the next time, or for the next believer he shall have to do with.[117]

One of the main instruments Satan uses in this operation against the Christian, surprising as it may seem, is false reasonings about the content of Scripture. Richard Gilpin has noticed this, and in the same work previously quoted writes:

> His way is not only to suggest that they are unregenerate, or under an evil frame of heart, but to offer proof that these accusations are true. And because he hath to do with them that profess a belief of Scripture, as the oracles of God, he will fetch his proofs from thence, telling them that he will evidence what he saith from Scripture. Thus sometimes he assaults the weaker, unskilful sort of Christians: 'Thou art not a child of God, for they that are so are enlightened, translated from darkness, they are the children of light; but thou art a poor ignorant dark blind creature, therefore no child of God . . .' whereas the ignorance which the man complains of is not the ignorance which those Scriptures intend.[118]

And so, 'whilst he is pouring upon his defects, Satan claps an arrest upon him of a far greater debt than God chargeth upon him'.[119]

Sometimes, Gilpin continues, Satan tries to convince the Christian soul that it is unregenerate 'from the infirmities of God's children, abusing to this purpose that of 1 John 3:9 "He that is born of God doth not commit sin", and that "he cannot sin because he is born of God" '[120] whereas 'the miscarriages of infirmity which the child of God laments in himself are not the same with that of the text upon which Satan grounds the accusation'.[121] Thus, Gilpin concludes, both here and wherever Satan misuses the Scriptures to bring the Christian soul into despair, 'the fallacy lies in the misapplying of the Scriptures . . . under a sense which was never intended by them',[122] and the success often gained by Satan is due to the natural reverence for God's word in the Christian soul, because of which the tempted souls 'are not willing to suspect the sense' which the Devil puts on to it. Another of Satan's instruments is to induce false reasonings about God. 'In this,' asserts Gilpin, 'Satan directly crosseth the design of the Scriptures, where God, in his nature and dealings is so set forth, that the weakest, the most afflicted and tossed, may receive encouragement of acceptance, and of his fatherly care over them in their saddest trials. Yet withal, lest men should turn his grace into wantonness, and embolden themselves in sin because of his clemency, the Scriptures sometimes give us lively descriptions of his anger against those that wickedly presume upon his goodness and continue so to do. Both these descriptions of God should be taken together, as affording the only true representations of him. . . . Now Satan will sometimes argue against the children of God, and endeavour to break their hopes by turning that part of the description of God against them which is intended for the dismounting of the confidence of the wicked and the bringing down of high looks . . . and in the meantime hiding that part of it that speaks God's wonderful condescensions, infinite compassions, unspeakable readiness to accept the broken hearted.'[123]

Satan further uses as a tool false reasonings about sin. First of all, observes Gilpin, 'Satan, with a kind of feigned ingenuity', will admit 'a difference betwixt sin and sin, betwixt sins reigning and not reigning; sins mortified and not mortified; betwixt the sins of the converted and the unconverted; and upon this supposition he usually proceeds. He doth not always (except in case of great sins) argue want of regeneration from one sin, for that argument . . . would be easily answered . . . but he thus deals with men: "These sins whereof thou art guilty, are reigning sins, such as are inconsistent with a converted estate, and therefore thou art yet unregenerate" '.[124] Gilpin confesses that the difference between sins in the elect and others is 'a very difficult case', the only final answer to which must be that, 'the difference betwixt the one and the other must depend upon the secret powers of grace giving check to these infirmities and striving to mortify them'.[125]

The most prominent detectable signs of this include, says Gilpin: '(1) Hatred of sin before the commission of it: "What I hate, that do I." (2) Reluctancy in the act: "What I would that I do not." (3) Disallowance after the act: "That which I do I allow not."[126] Yet seeing that emotions similar to these may be produced by common as distinct from saving grace, Satan still dogs conscience-stricken believers who complain: 'If our sins were but the usual failings of the converted, we might comfort ourselves; but they are great, they are backslidings, they are against conscience, they are many; what can we judge but that we have hitherto deceived ourselves, and that the work of conversion is yet to do.'[127]

No complaint drew from the Puritan pastor more ready or more gracious comfort than this, and another writer of that day, Thomas Harrison, is entirely typical, and surpassingly clear and luminous when he resorts to such troubles of soul in his book *Topica Sacra, or Spiritual Logick*. Conceiving backsliding to be most immediately sins against the third Person of the Trinity, he directs the enquirer to 'go to' the Spirit and

> Ask him if it be possible for thee to be in a worse plight than when he had first to do with thee? And did he then fall to work upon thee when he might have abhorred to foul his fingers with thee, and will he now forsake the work of his own hands? Ps. 138:8.[128]

Further, Harrison bids his enquirer turn to the Scriptures and argue from them: 'Were not all those gracious tenders to back-sliders framed, filled and recorded by him? Jer. 3:22 "Return ye backsliding children, and I will heal your backslidings": "Behold we are come to thee, for thou art the Lord our God"; Hosea 14:4 "I will heal their backslidings, I will love them freely, for mine anger is turned away from them"; and in many other places; and beg he would teach thee experimentally to know what is meant by God's healing backsliding.'[129] Again, Harrison's advice to the tormented believer is to turn to God the Son, and remind himself that 'the wisdom which is from above is gentle and easy to be entreated (Jas. 3:17), and shalt thou not find the essential Wisdom of the Father to be so? Is it so where there is but a drop, and not so where there is the whole ocean'?[130] And turning thus to Christ, the Christian is to,

> Plead what Christ himself puts into thy mouth (Matt. 18:13), that the owner of the flock looks with more joy and pleasure and delight upon a poor stray sheep that is recovered, than upon the whole flock that never ran that hazard. . . . 'Tis a recovering church and people which Christ is so taken with . . . one that hath been forsaken and desolate, whom the Lord is said to delight in, Is. 62:4 . . . 'tis to a reforming people that the Lord engageth that all nations shall call them blessed . . . (Mal. 3:2). . . . 'Tis a repaired, a re-edified temple, that the Lord promiseth to take pleasure in, Hag. 1:8.[131]

Finally, Harrison directs, the believer is to look to the Father at such times of assault, and that without fear, for: 'Doth not the sweet savour of Christ's sacrifice, the odour of his intercession, so diffuse

Thomas Manton D.D.

*All Puritan lovers know Manton's 'Long-metre version' of
Psalm 119—preached in 190 sermons! Most would agree
with C. H. Spurgeon's words 'There is not a poor discourse in
the whole collection: he is evenly good, constantly excellent.
Ministers who do not know Manton need not wonder if they are
themselves unknown.' To Manton and his fellows, the verbal
inspiration of Scripture was more than a theory.*

Viri verè Reverendi
JOSEPHI CARYL
Vera Effigies.

*Joseph Caryl.   Leading figure and preacher among the
Independents, he fathered the colossal 12-volume Commentary
upon Job—the result of 25 years preaching on that one book.
Among lesser men it has become a legend of prolixity—it is in
fact a monument to the fulness of Scripture and the vigour of the
Puritan pulpit.*

itself and fill heaven, that the stench of thy sins cannot enter?'[132]
And so, looking to the Father, the Christian is to:

> Ask whether he look on thee as in thy present state and station,
> or as he shall see thee (after a little while) to all eternity? For to
> him . . . there is nothing past nor to come, but all things are alike
> in one perpetual *now*, present before him. Now within a while,
> Christ will 'present to himself' . . . and to his Father, 'a glorious
> church, not having spot or wrinkle, nor any such thing, but holy and
> without blemish' (Eph. 5:27); and if now he viewed thee in that
> eternal glass, he may well say 'Thou art fair my love, there is no spot
> in thee' (Cant. 4:7).[133]

False reasonings about grace provide for Satan a powerful weapon
against the Christian. Richard Gilpin neatly summarises Satan's
wiles in this respect, when he points out that here Satan 'heightens
grace in the notion or abstract all he can', and 'lessens it in the
concrete or practice as much as is possible'.[134] With regard to the
former, Gilpin assures us: 'We may be sure . . . he will not stick to
give false definitions of grace and to tell a man that it is what indeed
it is not. . . . So, when Satan comes to describe grace, he sets it
forth in its highest excellencies and most glorious attainments . . .
and tells them if they have not that, they have nothing.'[135] Along
this same line, Satan 'gives us a description of grace as it is *in itself*,
abstracted from the weakness, dullness, distraction and infirmities
that are concomitant with it as it comes forth to practice . . . whereas
indeed, a true Christian may be found sometimes evidently practis-
ing one grace, and weak, or at present defective, in another. And
sometimes the best of his graces is so interrupted with temptations,
so clogged with infirmity, that its workings are scarce discernible'.[136]
Following on from this is Satan's lessening of grace in practice.
'This,' avers Gilpin, 'is the centre of his design,' and he suggests
that this attack comes from three main directions:

> 1. He compares the present state of anyone with whom he deals,
> to the highest attainments and excellencies of grace, allowing
> nothing to be grace but what will answer these descriptions . . . tells
> them what grace is at the highest, but not a word of what it is at the
> lowest. . . .
> 2. Another part of his cunning . . . is to take them at a disadvantage
> when their graces are weakest, and themselves most out of order.
> He that will choose to measure a man's stature while he is upon his
> knees, seems not to design to give a faithful account of his height: no
> more does Satan, who, when he will make comparisons, always takes
> the servants of God at the worst.[137]

Yet another stratagem is used, when Satan tries to convince the
fearful Christian that he never was truly regenerate, urging him

'with the possibility, nay, a probability of their mistaking themselves by passing too favourable an opinion formerly of their actions. To confirm them in this apprehension, (i) he lays before them the consideration of the deceitfulness of the heart (Jer. 17:6)',[138] with the result that 'the party doth not know, but his heart might deceive him in all that he hath done: which the Devil yet further endeavoureth to confirm, (ii) by a consideration of the seeming holiness and graces of such as believed themselves to be the children of God, and were generally by others reputed so to be, who yet after a glorious profession turned apostates'.[139]

A weighty answer to Satan's argument from Jeremiah 17:9 and the deceitfulness of the heart even in the regenerate, is given by the celebrated Nathaniel Culverwell, in his treatise on assurance, *The White Stone*. Culverwell insists that the Christian is able truly to assess the truth of grace (however small), or the lack of it in his heart, despite the waywardness of the heart, else, 'Why are Christians so often enjoined to try their own hearts, to search their own spirits, if that after all their diligence they cannot tell what to think of them'?[140] He agrees with William Ames, that there is a certain 'gift of discernment (donum discretionis) which Christians have by which they can discern true grace from counterfeit' in their own hearts. As for the argument for uncertainty drawn from examples of those who eventually apostastise, Culverwell is refreshingly bluff, and almost laughs the soul out of the fears with which Satan has surrounded it:

> One man's self-deceit does not prejudice another's certainty. What if one man flatter himself in a false light, and please himself in a mere shadow of assurance; must all men needs follow his example? A man that is in a dream, thinks himself awake when he is not: aye, but (I hope) for all this, a man that is awake, may certainly know that he is so. Many a traveller has thought himself in a right way when he has been out of it: and yet this does not hinder but that he that is well acquainted with the road may know that he is in his way. . . . One man's folly and vanity does not at all hinder another's assurance.[141]

The second main area of assault where Satan uses and increases spiritual depressions and desertions in Christians, appears in much of Puritan literature as:

(b) Using guilt of conscience

Conscience shares in the effects of the fall of man as truly as any

other part of the human constitution, and accordingly, even in the
regenerate, the conscience is not infallible or unerring. Writes
Joseph Symonds: 'An erroneous conscience, as sometimes it errs by
exacting less than it should, and giving acquittance when the debt
is not fully discharged, so sometimes it errs by going beyond its
commission and exacting above the bond . . . the spirit of a man is
so apt to err, that like water which is hardly kept within its bounds,
if it transgress not on the left hand by defect, it often mistakes on
the right hand by excess.'[142]

Satan, therefore, uses this in tempting a wounded spirit to despair,
and, offering false considerations and logic, feeds the conscience such
mis-information that its judgment becomes warped, and its conclusions harmful. This process is described in typically Puritan fashion
by Thomas Goodwin. Goodwin demonstrates how, in the manner
of a syllogism, Satan advances from a major premise, through a
minor premise, to a shattering conclusion. Goodwin exposes the
fallacy of one or other of Satan's premises and thus, of his conclusion:

> Satan oft argueth and chargeth the conscience of one distressed,
> in this or the like manner: 'Those in whom any sin reigneth, or in
> whose hearts hypocrisy or self-love is the predominant principle, are
> not in a state of grace. But such a one art thou' etc. In which sort
> of reasoning the major and first proposition is true; but the minor,
> the assumption, such a one art thou, that is most false. And al-
> though there be a truth in the instances alleged to prove it . . . yet
> not in that manner as would lay the charge, not as reigning, not as
> the swaying and prevailing principle in a man's whole course. . . .
> The deceit . . . lies chiefly in the assumption and minor proposition;
> that is, in misapplication to a man's self.[143]

Satan's minor premise here, 'such a one art thou', with its own
often specious 'proofs', is countered well by William Spurstowe,
who teaches the Christian to be wary before conceding anything
by way of admission to the Devil in such arguments, and shows how
a careful definition can prevent a depressing conclusion: 'It is true
a child of God cannot be a hypocrite, but he may have hypocrisy in
him.'[144] Therefore the believer must distinguish between sin
troubling and even sometimes raging in the soul, and the far different
case of sin reigning as the 'swaying and prevailing principle' in that
soul. The latter is incompatible with a state of grace, the former
is not.

Here it may be as well to note Thomas Goodwin's valuable aside
concerning the difference between the sometimes sharp, reproving
searchings and trials of the Holy Spirit, and those of the devil: the
great difference being that 'the Holy Ghost dealeth sweetly herein . . .

as a father that rebukes and convinceth his child of his misde-
meanours; but without putting in any such sting in the conclusion
that therefore we are hypocrites, nor . . . that therefore sin reigns
in us etc: but in these of Satan, that is the issue he mainly drives
all to'.[145]   Christopher Love sums it up in his own way when he
describes the difference as the difference between Christ's fan and
the Devil's sieve: 'Now the use of the sieve is contrary to the fan, for
that keeps the waste and lets out the best,' even so, Satan, by stirring
up a scrupulous conscience 'doth all he can to destroy our grace, and
to increase our sin'.[146]

Finally, and as an important remedy to all this, another writer,
Samuel Annesley, notable as a leader among the Puritans of his
day, recommends such a Christian as has been described, whose
conscience has been assailed and overwhelmed by Satan, to:

> Do what possibly you can to get rid of your scruples: but if you
> cannot get rid of them, *act* against them.   It is not only lawful, but
> necessary to go against a scrupulous conscience, or you will never
> have either grace or peace.   Should a Christian forbear praying, or
> receiving the sacrament every time his scrupulous conscience tells
> him, he . . . would soon find out to . . . [his] . . . sorrow, the mis-
> chief of [his] . . . scruples. . . .   Be resolute therefore, and tell the
> Devil, that as you do not perform your duty at his command, so
> neither will you omit it at his bidding.[147]

And then, delightfully:

> Do by religious duties, as they that are afraid to go by water, or
> to go over a narrow bridge – they cease to fear when they have gone
> often over: so, by the performance of duties, your scrupulous fears
> will vanish. . . .   In short, in all necessary, known duties, always do
> what you can, when you cannot do what you would.[148]

It should be added at this point, that in most Puritan treatments
of Satan's assaults on the conscience of a depressed Christian, the
advice of a mature Christian, and especially a faithful pastor, who
would be able to reassure the Christian of his essentially good standing in grace, was enjoined.   As Simon Ford observes: 'A stander-by
(say we) oftentime sees more than the parties in action can see
themselves.'[149]

A third area of Satanic assault follows:

(c) Using human emotions

Few Christians suffering desertion and depressions escape Satan's
attack upon the emotions, either to a greater or a lesser degree.

Most Puritan writers here agree that Satan cannot work directly upon either the conscience or the emotions (affections, to use the old word), but can only arouse and increase fears and depressions mediately and indirectly, using either the person's natural inclinations or circumstances, or else capitalising on present spiritual troubles with false suggestions. So, observes Goodwin, Satan can 'stir and work upon the passions' and 'make use of them' to insinuate 'hideous and horrid fears and terrors'. In this way he 'augments our fears and griefs, and causeth such disquietments and pangs'; and though 'God . . . alone knows, and can immediately wound the spirit and conscience', yet, Satan can and does 'terrify weak consciences that are ensnared with the cords of their own sins, by reason of the terrors which he hath received from the Lord' and can 'increase in us the fears of . . . death, by presenting to us the terrors of the law'. Finally he can 'immediately and by his own power stir the [already present] passions of fear and grief etc., excite them beyond nature, as the wind can raise the billows of the sea . . . and so can cause such thunders and lightnings as shall hurl all into black confusion, such as if hell and the soul would presently come together'.[150] Thus, though Satan cannot light the fire, he can and does blow up the flame.

Richard Gilpin has traced for us in some detail Satan's operations in this area. Among the chief ingredients of these spiritual-emotional distresses, he lists the following:

1. There is usually a complication of several kinds of troubles. Sometimes there are outward troubles, and inward discomposures of spirit arising from thence; sometimes affrightments of blasphemous thoughts long continued; and usually spiritual troubles (in which their state or condition have been called to question) have gone before.[151]

Gilpin here cites Heman, in Psalm 88, as 'as famous an instance in this case as any we meet withal in Scriptures'.

2. These troubles drive at a further end than any of the former; for their design was only against the present quietness and peace of God's children, but these design the ruin of their hopes for the future; they are troubled, not for that they are unconverted, but for that they expect never to be converted.
3. These troubles have the consent and belief of the party. In some other troubles . . . they opposed, and refused to give consent: but in these Satan prevails with them to believe that their case is really such as their fears represent it to be.
4. These are troubles of a far higher degree than the former: the deepest sorrows, the sharpest fears, the greatest agonies. Heman, Ps. 88:15,16, calls them 'terrors' even to 'distraction'.[152]

Although the remedy for such situations will appear under 'The Cure of Spiritual Desertions and Depressions', it is as well to recollect Richard Gilpin's observations here: 'I have endeavoured to show,' he writes, 'the methods of the Tempter, which is no small help to preserve men from being thus imposed upon, and to recover out of his snare those that are,' for "tis a great preservative from sickness, and no mean advantage to the cure, to have a discovery of the disease and causes of it.' He concludes: 'Let none be afraid of this Goliath; let no man's heart faint because of him. A fear of caution and diligence to avoid his snares is a necessary duty . . . but a discouraging, distrustful fear is a dishonourable reflection upon God's power and promises to help us, and upon the Captain of our Salvation, who goeth out before us. Let us hold on in the practice of holiness, and not be afraid. The God of peace shall tread down Satan under our feet shortly. Amen.'[153]

(iv) When he does it

Gilpin has some fine observations on this point, and without quoting any other Puritan authors on what was a favourite subject of theirs, we list his six principal periods in the Christian life when Satan especially seeks to increase depression to the point of despair.

1. The time of conversion . . . at this time he can easily overdrive them. Where the convictions are deep and sharp, ready to weigh them down, a few grains more cast in the scale will make the trouble (as Job speaks) 'heavier than the sand'.

2. The time of solemn repentance for some great sin committed after conversion . . . thence follow fear, shame, self-indignation, bitter weeping, deep humiliation; then comes Satan: he rakes their wounds . . . pours in corrosives instead of oil, and all to make them believe that their spot is not the spot of God's children . . . at which time the Adversary is very busy to work up their hearts to excess of fear and sorrow. This was the course which he took with the incestuous Corinthian, taking advantage of his great transgressions 'to overwhelm him with too much sorrow' (2 Cor. 2:7,11).

3. Satan watcheth the discomposures of the spirits of God's children under some grievous cross or affliction . . . David seldom met with outward trouble but he at the same time had a conflict with Satan about his spiritual condition or state.

4. When Satan hath prepared the hearts of God's children by atheistical or blasphemous thoughts, he takes that occasion to deny their grace and interest [share] in Christ. And the argument at that time seems unanswerable: 'Can Christ lodge in a heart so full of horrid blasphemies against him? Is it possible it should be washed

and sanctified, when it produces such filthy and accursed thoughts?'[154]

Gilpin's fifth 'solemn occasion' when Satan tempts thus, is at times of 'melancholy', which, in Puritan terminology, as we have seen, generally means natural and nervous depression as distinct from spiritual depression. 'Few persons,' he writes, 'distempered therewith, do escape Satan's hands,' and 'no wonder' since 'melancholy affects both head and heart . . . the heart trembles, and the head is darkened . . . every object is mis-represented'; the heart is 'strong in its fears', and the understanding misinforming its judgment, 'is strong in its mistakes'. Moreover, 'these impressions are usually lasting', and often continue 'for months and years'. When the Christian is thus broken under mental distress, Satan has merely by 'altering the object' of their attentions and fears to turn that attention to their soul's state or everlasting destiny 'and he hath a spiritual distress'.[155]

Finally, and as his sixth 'occasion', Gilpin quotes 'sickness, or death-bed experiences':

'We may truly call sickness and death-bed an 'hour of temptation', which Satan will make use of with the more mischievous industry because he hath but a short time for it. . . . So that in this case Satan encourageth himself to the battle with 'now or never'. And hence we find that it is usual for the dying servants of God to undergo most sharp encounters [when Satan tells them], that they are yet in their blood, without God, without hope [and this], is enough to affright them into the extremist agonies for they see no time before them answerable to so great a work if it be yet to do. And withal, they are under vast discouragements from the weariness and pains of sickness, their understandings and faculties being also dull and stupefied.[156]

Nevertheless, Gilpin expresses his conviction that God, at such times, generally pacifies the troubled Christian in a direct and often surprising manner, supporting this view with his own experience of many cases.

(c) THE CURE OF SPIRITUAL DESERTIONS AND DEPRESSIONS

SOME BASIC PRINCIPLES

The Puritans never recognised a spiritual malady in Christian experience that was not to some extent, and at some stage, curable. They insisted that spiritual depressions and desertion could be, and should be in great measure, alleviated by sound counsel wisely applied and properly taken, and that it was a major part of ministerial faithfulness for the pastor to be able to give such counsel. From the outset they established and re-established, that as grace was the unmerited favour of the immutable God, then it too was as unchangeable as was its Giver, in its existence in the soul of the believer, even if its powers and effects varied, for 'the gifts and calling of God' were 'without repentance'.

The Puritans loved to descant upon the indissolubleness of the believer's election, the inviolability of his standing and the certainty of his eternal state in glory: and they applied these principles with vigour and graciousness to the depressed Christian. Joseph Symonds does this when he counsels:

> Desertions are not the interruptions of God's love, but of the acts of his love; his affection is the same, but the expression is varied . . . Ps. 89:30,34. . . . When God deserts his people, he withholds those acts of love only that are for our well-being, not those which are for our being. Though a Christian may want [lack] that without which he cannot have peace, yet not that without which he cannot live . . . Ps. 84:11.[157]

As Thomas Goodwin explains: 'The real gracious influences and effects of his favour may be continued, upholding, strengthening and carrying on the soul still to obey and fear him, whilst he yet conceals his favour. For when Christ complained, "My God, my God, why hast thou forsaken me"? . . . he never more obeyed God, was never stronglier supported than at that time.'[158] No one has put it more plainly than Matthew Lawrence in his *Use and Practice of Faith*, who assures the humbled Christian in this position:

> God may withdraw from his people such graces as are called accessory graces, but not such graces as are absolutely necessary. . . . Sometimes God doth forsake his people when his people forsake him by falling from their 'first love', and from their first degree of zeal, Gal. 4:15. But God doth never forsake his people so far as to suffer them to fall altogether from those necessary graces which tend to the very being of a Christian. . . . Justification, and Adoption and the Spirit of Regeneration abide for ever.[159]

Lawrence, therefore, counsels the troubled Christian to live by faith in and through such dark periods, 'For though *communion* with God may be debarred for a time, yet *union* is unchangeable (Heb. 13:5,6).'[160]

Working from this most basic principle, Christopher Love, in his already much-quoted *Dejected Soul's Cure*, lays down nine considerations why the troubled soul should not be too cast down, and in so doing, gathers up much that has been said on this whole matter earlier in the book:

1. Consider that God's withholding the sense of his love and favour from the soul is not always an act of justice for to punish them for sin, but sometimes an act of sovereignty.
2. God may withdraw his love and favour from the soul, not from any displeasure that he hath to them, but out of an act of love to try his own people's love to him; as a mother, a tender-hearted mother, many times runs behind the door from her child in a corner, and hides herself, but it is not because she is angry with her child, but to try the strength of her child's love in seeking after the mother.
3. God may suspend his favour because there may be more of God's fatherly love in withdrawing his love, than in manifesting his love . . . and that in these two particulars: (i) When a man doth enjoy the sense of God's love and that enjoyment makes him spiritually proud. . . . A little boat cannot bear a great sail without sinking . . . many times the enjoyment of a comfort makes you to grow secure and to grow careless . . . God doth sometimes forsake that so he might not be forsaken . . . (ii) The suspension of God's love and favour is in love, when it doth make them to prize Jesus Christ more in the want of him, than thou didst in the enjoyment of him.
4. That you may not be too much cast down, consider that the people of God have always *ground* of comfort in their souls, though they have not always *sense* of comfort; as a man hath a right to an inheritance, though he cannot read the evidences of it.
5. Remember this for thy support, that none of God's children do retain always the like sense of manifestations of God's love to their souls, but it fares with the souls of God's people in reference to comfort as it is with the sea: the sea sometimes ebbing and sometimes flowing; and as with the air: sometimes cloudy and sometimes clear; and so like the seasons of the year: sometimes winter and sometimes summer. As it is in nature, so it is in grace: no child of God under heaven doth always at all times retain and keep the same measure of comforts in his own spirit.
6. If at any time God doth suspend his love and favour, and the light of his countenance, yet consider that God never doth this but he seeth great reason and need for it. . . . If you need heaviness, you shall have heaviness; if no need of sorrow, you shall have no sorrow. Philosophers say there is great need of wind and thunder, as well as of shining of the sun, for thereby the air is kept clear; so, when God doth thunder into thy soul, and sometimes bluster like wind into thy soul, God doth see some need of that dealing with thee, to sweep thy soul from sin and the love of the world, and quell thy pride . . . and sometimes God may do it to stir up in thee a compassionate spirit toward others in affliction.
7. Consider . . . that Jesus Christ himself, was under spiritual desertion as well as thou: Christ himself cried, 'My God, my God, why hast thou forsaken me?', Matt. 27:46. Here was *subtractio visionis*, though not *unionis*.

8. Consider this, that the seeming loss of God's favour is not simply prejudicial to the state of grace, for it doth not hinder thy having access to, and having success at the throne of grace, neither can it hinder thee of glory . . . it is the want of Christ, not of comfort, that makes the throne of grace a throne of justice and wrath . . . it is the truth of grace, and not the sense and sight of grace, that brings the soul to heaven.

9. Consider, when you come to heaven, you shall have comfort enough; God doth reserve the fulness of thy comfort until the fulness of thy glory. . . .   Here in this world, joy . . . entereth into you, but in the world to come you shall enter into joy.[161]

After such considerations, one can appreciate that it was with a considered seriousness that another writer, William Bridge, could say (and the sentiment is typically Puritan) 'Surely, therefore, you have no reason for your discouragements *whatever* your desertions be'.[162]

Thus did the Puritan pastor lay the foundations for comfort to the afflicted soul.   Nevertheless, such sacred foundations were not laid for indiscriminate use, and it will be salutary to attend to some cautionary notes sounded by the Puritan divines on the use and application of these comforts, with some warnings ('caveats', to use the fine old word) to the pastor dealing with spiritual depressions and desertions.

One of the most sustained and prominent Puritan assaults against those who too easily apply facile comfort to men's hearts, is launched by Robert Bolton of Kettering in his *Instructions for a Right Comforting of Afflicted Consciences*.   In a two-hundred-page section of the work, he marshalls a formidable array of quotations from patristic, medieval and Puritan authorities, in order to show that the precious comforts of the covenant of grace should not be administered indiscriminately; for example to such as: (i) The unconverted. (ii) Those whose depression is caused by outward trouble, and not inward sin.   (iii) Those who confess sin in general, but have no sufficient conviction of sins in particular (such persons being out of love with sin in the abstract, but not with sins in concrete, and therefore not truly out of love with sin at all).   (iv) Those who are troubled for one 'notorious' sin, but neglect the rest.   (v) Those who have only such troubles on their death-beds, and out of a natural fear rather than a spiritual conviction.[163]

Also, such comforts must not be weakened by being administered either too soon (before the trouble is properly rooted out), or too much (*ie.* in such a way that the beginnings of an understanding of faith degenerate into presumption).   And it was very necessary that the faithful physician of troubled souls use his knowledge with care and discretion, lest he cheapen the commodity and largely neutralise the potential good which his counsel could do. Therefore, Bolton's summary applies as well to the converted as to the unconverted when he bids the counselling minister to proceed by 'pressing the law – promising mercy – proposing Christ', and so to give the whole counsel of God its due place that it might have its full effect.[164]

One caution more should be mentioned here, namely, that the troubled soul must not necessarily expect a full recovery immediately. Such a caution can prevent an early relapse, and Joseph Caryl lays it down as a doctrine that 'The Lord doth usually raise his people by degrees', and continues:

> As it is with men that have long pined with famine and hunger, and are grown out of their ordinary course by reason of their necessitated abstinence, we do not presently give them all manner of good cheer, or bring them to a full table, and let them eat as much as they will, but we give them a little and a little at a time, and so, by degrees, bring their stomachs on till they be wrought for plenty; so, when the Lord brings persons or nations very low, he doth not bring in a glut of mercies at first, this would be more than they are able to bear, as they may be undone if they have all at one receipt; but he gives as they are able to take them in, and make a right use of them. . . . We may be over-mercied as well as over-afflicted, over-laden with comforts as well as with sorrows. And therefore, as the Lord doth correct with judgement, and in a measure, so alas doth he restore. We have not full tide in a moment, or in a quarter of an hour: it would be terrible, dangerous and troublesome, if when it is low water we should have full tide in a moment, but it comes in stealing by degrees, and at last it swells all over the banks. Such a stealing flood of mercies the Lord gives his people.
> Therefore be cautioned. In the returns of mercy, do not despise small things. Your beginnings may be inconsiderable – this is but a little and that is but a little – but do not despise the first or second little. So the prophet counsels (Zech. 4:10) 'Despise not the day of small things'.[165]

Having laid some first principles in counselling the condition of spiritual desertions and depression, it is now time to turn to the range of positive advice given by the Puritan pastors to souls labouring under the malady.

SOME DIRECTIONS

(i) Fly to God

Richard Sibbes has written finely on this point in his book *The Soul's Conflict*. Recognising how imperative it is when in deep darkness of soul to go to God, and yet understanding with a true pastor's heart that this is the very thing most difficult to do at such times, Sibbes, in considering Psalm 42, 'where David commands his soul, Hope thou in God', asks, 'But how came David to have the command of his own soul, so as to take it off from grief, and to place it upon God?' and answers:

> The child of God hath something in him above a man; he hath the spirit of God to guide his spirit. This command of David to his soul was under the command of the Great Commander. God commands David to trust in him, and at the same time infuseth strength into his soul . . . to command itself to trust God.[166]

Thus did David have 'a double superior above him: his own spirit as sanctified, and God's Spirit guiding that'. Therefore:

> Let but David say to his soul, being charged of God to trust, 'I charge thee my soul to trust him', and he finds a present strength enabling to it. Therefore, we must both depend upon God as the first mover, and withal set all the inferior wheels of our souls agoing according as the Spirit of God ministers motion unto us. So shall we be free from self-confidence, and likewise from neglecting that order of working which God hath established.[167]

Sibbes has no doubt that this will be demonstrated in the tried Christian's experience, for he lays it down as a sure truth that, 'There is a sanctified use of all troubles to God's children: first, they drive them out of themselves, and then draw them nearer to God'. Therefore, 'Let not Christians muse so much upon their troubles, but see whither it carries them. . . . It is a never-failing rule of discerning a man to be in the state of grace, when he finds every condition draw him nearer to God'.[168]

Joseph Symonds encourages the depressed Christian thus drawn or driven to his God for relief not to fear the outcome of his Father-ward flight from depression: 'You have a right to peace and comfort, for it is that which Christ died for, and which he hath left as a legacy to his people: "Peace I leave with you, my peace give I unto you" (John 14:27). Sit not therefore under discouragements . . . but reach after that which is before you.'[169]

In this 'reaching after God', the same writer makes a great point of using the mediation of Christ: 'Seek the Father in the Son:

haply you have not held up Christ in your hearts, and for your strangeness to the Son, the Father hath estranged himself; go and carry Christ in your arms, for he is dear unto him, and the Father hath determined to pour out all his love through the Son. . . . The Father's mercies melt at the Son's mediation.'[170]

Thomas Goodwin presses home the lesson when he writes:

> Above all things *pray*; and get others to pray for thee. . . . This counsel the apostle gives you, Jas. 5:13, 'Is any man afflicted? Let him pray'. And because, of all afflictions else, this of darkness in a man's spirit needeth prayer the most . . . this, says David, is my constant practice: 'when my soul is overwhelmed, I pour out my prayer unto Thee' Ps. 61:2. . . . And if through all these discouragements thy condition prove worse and worse, so as thou canst not pray, but art struck dumb when thou comest into his presence, as David Ps. 77:4, 'I am so troubled I cannot speak', then fall a-making signs when thou canst not speak: groan, sigh, sob and 'chatter', as Hezekiah did; bemoan thyself for thine own unworthiness, and desire Christ to speak thy requests for thee, and God to hear him for thee. Christ, he is 'an advocate with the Father', 1 John 2:1, and pleads no bad case, nor was ever cast [defeated] in any suit he pleaded.[171]

(ii) Trust in God

'Learn to trust in a withdrawing God,' writes Thomas Manton, 'and depend upon him; to stay ourselves upon his name when we see no light, Isa. 50:10. Never leave until you find him. Look, as Esther would go into the king's presence when there was no golden sceptre held forth, so, venture into God's presence when you have no smile and countenance from heaven; trust in a withdrawing God: nay, when wrath breaks out, when God killeth you: Job 13:15 "Though he kill me, yet will I trust in him". With such a holy obstinacy of faith should we follow God in this case.'[172]

'Let me tell thee,' adds Thomas Goodwin after a similar paragraph, 'such a resolution can never go to hell with thee.'[173] Richard Sibbes, in entire harmony with his fellow-Puritans, writes in his *Discouragement's Recovery*: 'This trusting in God is the way to quiet our souls, and to stay the same in every estate. The reason is, because God hath sanctified this holy grace to this end.'[174] In another work, the same writer, with happy ingenuity encourages his readers to exercise this trust on its 'only fit object', when he writes: 'A man can be in no condition wherein God is at a loss and cannot

help him. If comforts be wanting, he can create comforts, not
only out of nothing, but out of discomforts!'[175]

If it be enquired on what grounds the believer can so trust in
times of depression, two great reasons appear. Matthew Lawrence
has already provided the first in his observation quoted earlier:
'Though communion with God may be debarred for a time, yet
union is unchangeable.' The second warrant or ground of trust is
given in some detail by Goodwin. Goodwin has largely been
considering throughout his treatise the words of Isaiah 50:10, 'Who
is among you that feareth the Lord, that obeyeth the voice of his
servant, that walketh in darkness and hath no light? Let him trust
in the name of the Lord, and stay upon his God'. Here, he concludes:

> Thou mayest safely and confidently trust in and stay upon the
> name of God when thou hast nothing else to rest upon. . . . The
> name of God alone is here opposed to all other means and props
> which faith hath to rest on. It is opposed to all comfortable sense
> of God's love, to all sight of any grace in a man's self to which any
> promise is made. So that when the soul shall look into itself with
> one eye, and glance over all the word of God with another; and yet
> shall see not any one grace in the one, nor promise in the other made
> to any grace within itself which it may rest upon; yet the soul then
> looking upon God, and considering what a God he is, and what he
> says of himself, of his mercy and kindness, and free grace towards
> sinful men, even the sole consideration of what merely it knows to
> be in God, as he is revealed in the covenant of grace may support
> him. This is to stay upon his name.[176]

(a) Trust in his Son

Although one with the previous point, this was a qualification of
it in Puritan thought: for it was often of great help to the Christian
to think in terms of the Second Person of the Trinity distinctly,
when under spiritual depressions and desertion, and to direct trust
to him immediately, and thus to the Father in and through the Son.
Jeremiah Burroughs in a great treatise, *Christ Inviting Sinners to Come
to Him for Rest*, has written on this with great clarity:

> First labour to exercise thy faith upon Christ as one that was
> once in the same condition in some degree and some measure as
> thou art in . . . when he was upon the cross where he tells you
> plainly that he was forsaken, 'My God, my God, why hast thou
> forsaken me?' Thou thinkest that God hath withdrawn himself
> from thee? No, he will not withdraw himself from thee so much as
> from his Son . . . though still he had union with him by nature, and

he was his Father as before; but the human nature did not feel the influence of the grace and sweetness, and the shine of the favour of God as at other times. Exercise thy faith upon Christ as one that was in spiritual desertions . . . because that his being so forsaken, it was to sanctify thy being forsaken; it was to take away the curse of those desertions that thou hast in thyself. . . . There is no such way for the soul that is in spiritual desertions as to look up to Christ.

Secondly, if thou beest under the burden of spiritual desertions, then look up to Christ as being such a mediator as is full of grace and goodness; there being such a fulness of the grace of God in him, as makes him a sufficient object of the faith of adherence, when he cannot be unto me an object of the faith of evidence. . . . You will say, What is the meaning of that? I mean by the faith of evidence that I am able to say that Christ is mine, and I have an argument to persuade my conscience that he is mine; that is the faith of evidence. But yet, there is enough in Christ to draw forth the soul to rest upon him from the faith of adherence. That is thus: Though I cannot draw arguments to rely upon Christ as mine, yet I will cleave to him, and adhere to him; I know there is no help but there, and therefore will I cleave and cling; here now is the faith of adherence. Now because there is so much grace in it, therefore Christ may be a great object of thy faith of adherence, when thou canst not see him to be an object of the faith of evidence, and that is a way to help the soul in time of spiritual desertion.

Thirdly . . . the soul in this case is to exercise faith upon Christ as an advocate that is at the right hand of the Father to plead the cause of his people.

Fourthly: in thy spiritual desertion, thou must look up to Christ to seek the fulfilling of that promise of his that he makes to his disciples, to send them the Comforter.

Fifthly, in time of spiritual desertion, if thou canst find no evidence at all, nothing at all to satisfy thy soul, then go to Christ in the very same way thou wentest to him at first . . . thou art not in a worse condition than thou wast then, when thou wert an enemy, and thou foundest ease. . . . There are many people in time of spiritual afflictions and desertion, they spend so much time in looking after old evidences, whereas the truth is they might get new ones sooner than old ones, as sometimes a man may spend a great deal more time in looking after an old key of a box than in making a new one.

Sixthly, be sure in time of thy desertions to keep good thoughts of God, though thou hast no comfort in them for the present, yet believe it, there is comfort in Christ, and whatever becomes of thee, acknowledge Christ to be faithful, Christ to be thy Lord and thy king, and let thy heart love him. . . . And so in Ps. 88, the example of Heman, 'Oh God of my salvation': he still speaks well of God, and calls God the God of his salvation. . . . And so the Church in the Canticles when Christ . . . had withdrawn himself from her, yet she . . . would call him her beloved, and go up and down asking for her beloved and where her beloved was; so let the soul, in time of desertion. Keep good thoughts of God.[177]

Burroughs' final point refers to the temptation to escape from the situation by finding relief in the world, in sin or in any remedy outside of Christ: 'Seventhly and lastly: If thou canst not have rest in Christ, resolve thou wilt never find rest in ought else; that thy heart shall be restless 'till thou hast rest in Christ.'[178]

(b) Trust in his providence

It would be difficult to find a better definition of God's providence than that of Thomas Sharp, in his book *Divine Comforts, Antidoting Inward Perplexities of Mind.* Sharp writes: 'Providence is the transit of God's wisdom, power, justice, goodness, faithfulness, out of heaven and himself into the visible world: governing, protecting, caring for, directing and ordering all, for the most excellent ends worthy of God.' This gracious providence, as it is 'concerned for the catholic good, so in special for those that love God, and are the called according to his purpose, Rom. 8:28', and particularly 'to God's afflicted, tossed with tempest and not comforted (Isa. 54:11)' who 'are the peculiar care and charge of heaven'.[179]

But it may be objected at this stage that the same providence which protects us in distress is responsible in some measure for the distress. Richard Sibbes has written helpfully on this point, and, declaring that 'we are under a providence that is above our own', he gives us directions how we are to respond to such strange visitations which surround us with darkness of soul for a season. His first direction is that we 'lay our hands upon our mouths, and command the soul an holy silence, not daring to yield to the last rising of our hearts against God'. To make this advice good, he quotes David: 'I was dumb, and opened not my mouth because thou didst it' (Ps. 39:9) and Aaron (Lev. 10:1,2), adding: 'In this silence and hope is our strength, for God's ways seem oft to us full of contradictions because his course is to bring things to pass by contrary means.' Thus, 'when we are in heaven, it will be one part of our happiness to see the harmony of those things that seem now confused unto us'.[180]

Secondly, Sibbes counsels 'a holy resigning of ourselves to God', whose 'will is a wise will. . . . Thus David yields up himself to God: "Here I am; let the Lord deal with me as seemeth good unto him" 2 Sam. 15:26'.[181] Finally, Sibbes insists that 'The way patiently to suffer God's will, is to inure ourselves first to do it. Passive obedience springs from active'. This will bring our wills to

God's will for: 'We find by experience that when our wills are so subdued that we delight to do what God would have us do, and to be what God would have us be, that then sweet peace presently riseth to the soul.' In a word: 'Nothing should displease us that pleaseth God: neither should anything be pleasing to us that displeaseth him. This conformity is the ground of comfort.'[182]

Thomas Lye, in a Cripplegate sermon, puts it with characteristic Puritan wit: 'It is not fit that poor, weak, short-sighted, sinful creatures should be their own carvers. If they should, they would, like rash children, cut either too much, or too little, or their own fingers. Well for us, that as our times so our conditions are not in our own (but in God's) hands.'[183]

(c) Trust in his promises

Helpful as the previous remedy is, yet, 'for the better settling of our trust', Richard Sibbes informs us, 'God opened his heart to us in his Word, and reached out so many sweet promises for us to lay hold on. . . . For promises are, as it were, the stay of the soul in an imperfect condition, and so is faith in them, until all the promises shall end in performance, and faith in sight and hope in possession'.[184] Yet it is one of the most dismal features of a Christian in an extreme state of spiritual depression, that he feels unable, and even unwilling to lay hold on these promises put before him in the Scriptures for just such times. Thomas Goodwin places his finger on this sore spot when he recognises and rebukes those Christians whose depressions have so far perverted their judgment, 'so far distempered' their hearts, and so 'filled with anguish and sense of misery' their souls, 'that they reject all that is spoken for their comfort'. He continues:

> Tell them of what God hath wrought in them and for them as evidences of his love and . . . they pick quarrels and make objections at everything that is said, as if they were hired as lawyers to plead against themselves, and to find flaws in their evidences. I have observed some who have set all their wits a-work to strengthen all arguments and objections against themselves.[185]

Goodwin points to Asaph in Psalm 77 verses 2 and 10 as an example of this, and then rounding on Christians in such a perverse state warns: 'This sullen, peevish, desperate obstinacy is a thing you ought to take heed of; for hereby you take Satan's part . . . you give up your own right' in God's everlasting Covenant of Grace 'and you trust to lying vanities . . . of Satan and of your own hearts'.[186]

One of the most thorough of Puritan treatises on the promises of God in Scripture, is that by William Spurstowe: *The Wells of Salvation Opened*.[187] We shall take him for our guide here, in considering and applying the promises of Scripture as they apply to those in a depressed condition. Spurstowe establishes the need for the promises when he writes: 'Our knowledge, our graces, our comforts are all incomplete,'[188] for 'while we are here below, we are but as kings in the cradle: the throne on which we must sit, the robes with which we must be clothed, the crown which must be set upon our heads are all reserved for heaven.'[189] Therefore, all this is 'ratified and made sure' to us in the promises which 'seal heaven to believers in the other life and begin it in this life'.[190] These precious promises which so encourage a believer in this life, can, he assures us, never fail:

> But if at any time, these divine consolations do run in a more shallow and spare channel, and vary from their wonted fulness; yet do they never prove like the waters that fail or streams that are quite dried up. A believer may at some time be drawn low, but he can never be drawn dry. . . . His comforts may be like the widow's oil in the cruse, where only a little remains (1 Kgs. 17:12). . . . The Lord did put forth his power, though not in making the oil and meal to overflow . . . but in keeping it from wasting so as to be a constant supply unto her and the prophet's necessities in the extreme of famine.[191]

Even so, Spurstowe assures his readers, believers who are reduced to great extremities in outward trouble and inward weakness 'think they have scarce faith enough to last one day more, scarce strength enough for one prayer more, scarce courage enough for one conflict more . . . but in the midst of all these fears and misgivings which arise from their hearts, there issueth out such a measure of comfort from the promises, which, if it gives not deliverance from their temptations, doth effect their preservation in them; if it overflows not to make them *glad*, it fails not to make them *patient*, and to wait, "till God send forth judgment unto victory," Matt. 12:20'.[192]

Spurstowe's advice on how a Christian should use the promises of Scripture to relieve his soul in a depressed or deserted condition, takes many forms; but first he counsels:

(i) 'Eye God in the promises,' to which end he gives this salutary warning:

> Promises are not the primary object of faith, but the secondary:

or they are rather the means by which we believe, than the things
on which we are to rest. . . . The promises are instrumental in the
coming of Christ and the soul together; they are the *warrant* by which
faith is emboldened to come to him, and take hold of him; but the
union which faith makes, is not between a believer and the promise,
but between a believer and Christ.[193]

(ii) 'Eye free grace.' 'This direction,' Spurstowe assures us,
'touching the freeness of God's grace in the promises, is exceedingly
useful to succour and relieve the perplexing fears of the weak and
tempted Christian, who, though he have eyes to see the unspeakable
worth and excellency of the promises, yet hath not confidence to
put forth the hand of faith and to apply them to his own neces-
sities.'[194] Such a Christian, insists our author, must realise that the
promises of God 'are not made to such as deserve mercy, but to
such as want [desire] it', and that they spring 'not from any good
within us, but wholly from grace without us'. By a proper understanding of this, believers 'will readily find that by eyeing the
ground and original [origin] of the promise, they will sooner be
encouraged and drawn to believe and to lay hold upon it, than by
looking only to the promise itself'.[195] It is worth interjecting
Spurstowe's advice here, with a paragraph from William Bridge in
which he extends this principle: 'And if the promise does not come
to you, go you to it. Sometimes the promise comes to us, sometimes
we go to it. When the promise comes to you, you have joy; when
you go to it, you have peace, and this peace may last longer than
the joy. But remember this as an everlasting rule, that your very
relying upon the promise makes it yours.'[196]

Much of this is made most concrete in a succinct distinction from
scholastic divinity which Spurstowe approvingly quotes, and which
demonstrates that grace is most free to the believer, when it is most
bound by itself:

> Though the will of God be most entirely free in all his manifes-
> tations toward the creature, yet, upon the voluntary and free
> precedency of one supposed act, we may justly conceive him to be
> necessarily obliged to a second.[197]

Thus God was most absolutely free in the making of his promises,
but having made them, he is under a necessity to fulfil them by his
truth. In a word – Spurstowe's word – 'His promise hath made
him a debtor, but free grace made him a promiser'.[198]

After bidding us 'eye' God's power, God's immutability, God's
wisdom, all in some detail, Spurstowe offers the salutary and
constructive warning that such promises yet demand, for all their
freeness, a well-meaning, if weak effort on our part if we are to

enjoy their comfort: 'They are fulfilled not only in us, but by us,'[199] and 'the penny was given to the labourers in the vineyard, not to the loiterers in the market place'.[200] Spurstowe continues with another direction of note:

(iii) 'Meditate seriously and frequently on the promises.'[201] Here, in a passage worthy of Jeremy Taylor for sheer beauty, Spurstowe writes:

> I have sometimes thought that a believer's looking on a promise, is not unlike a man's beholding of the heavens in a still and serene evening, who, when he first casts up his eye, sees haply a star or two only to peep, and with difficulty to put forth a feeble and disappearing light. By and by, he looks up again, and both their number and lustre are increased. A while after, he views the heavens again, and then the whole firmament, from every quarter, with a numberless multitude of stars, is richly enamelled as with so many golden studs.
>
> So, when a Christian first turns his thoughts toward the promises, the appearances of light and comfort which shine from them, do oft times seem to be as weak and imperfect rays, which neither scatter fears nor darkness. When again he sets himself to ripen and improve his thoughts upon them, then the evidence and comfort which they yield to the soul is both clear and distinct: but when the heart and the affections are fully fixed in the meditation of a promise, Oh . . . what legions of beauties do then appear from every part of it which both ravish and fill the soul of the believer with delight![202]

Spurstowe continues:

(iv) 'Be much in the application of the promises. This dictum I propound the rather because that Christians, by lying under fears, darkness and temptations, are not seldom like hasty patients under diseases and infirmities, who, if they find not a present benefit in the use of physic, either in the removal or the abatement of their distempers, do straightways conclude that it were better for them to bear the pain of the disease, than to trouble themselves with the daily applications of fruitless remedies and prescripts, not considering that physic may be useful to . . . keep them from growing worse, though it do not make them better.'[203] There follows, in answer to the Christian whose trouble is such that every use of spiritual helps, including the promises, seems quickly to lose its effect, an anecdote illustrating the real and immediate efficacy of a sincere application of the promises of God to the depressed soul; an efficacy which is real even though it be not apparent:

> One of the fraternity came to the old Father, and complained, 'Father, I do often desire of the ancient Fathers some instructions for the good of my soul; and whatsoever they tell me, I forget all'. The

old man had two empty vessels, and bid him bring the one and pour water into it, and wash it clean and then pour out the water and set it up clean in its place; which, when the young man had accordingly done, he demanded: 'Which now of the two vessels is the more clean?' The young man answered, 'That into which I poured water and washed it'. Then replied the old Father, 'So is the soul which oftentimes heareth God's word, though it remembered not what it hath heard, yet it is more cleansed from sin than the soul that never comes to hear'.[204]

Later directions of Spurstowe's are:

(v) 'Make choice of some special promises to resort to in extremity.'[205] Frequent and concentrated familiarity with these will draw out their potency in a specially rich degree.

(vi) 'Be truly thankful for the least dawnings of mercy' which the promises at any time afford:

> The first glimmerings of peace and comfort which spring from the promises, are accompanied with a great mixture of darkness, but yet they are of a growing nature. . . . In the bestowing of his favours, God deals with believers as Boaz did with Ruth: he first gave her a liberty to glean in his fields; then invited her to eat bread at his table, and to dip her morsel in the vinegar; and lastly gave himself. So God first in a sparing manner and at some distance, makes a discovery of his love and good will unto them; then, in a more familiar manner and friendly way he encourageth them by his promise to draw near unto him, and to taste how good the Lord is to those who fear him; and then, as the complement of all, he gives his Spirit into their bosoms to assure them of his love, and their interest [share] in whatsoever might make them perfectly happy. 'After that ye believed, ye were sealed with that holy Spirit of promise,' saith the apostle, Eph. 1:13. But the ready and speedy way to obtain all this, is to be truly thankful for the least appearance of mercy that shines forth from the promises.[206]

'This direction,' Spurstowe concludes, 'I gladly would that those Christians should often have in their thoughts who are so much in complaining what they want [lack], that they never bless God for what they enjoy.'[207] Such believers should constantly remind themselves of one of Spurstowe's parting counsels, namely that 'the lowest estate that can befall a believer who hath an interest [share] and right' to the promises 'is far better than the brightest and most glorious condition of any person that can lay no claim or title to them'.[208]

Finally, it will be salutary here to make brief note of an important Puritan dictum well-expressed by Thomas Goodwin. To his 'child of light walking in darkness', and as such, unwilling to claim many of the rich promises of God's word, Goodwin counsels a true and

honest searching of the heart and its experience for just one feature
which has a promise of grace made to it: 'For if one promise do
belong to thee, then all do; for every one conveys [the] whole Christ
in whom all the promises are made and who is the matter of them. . . .
And if thou canst say, as the Church in Ephesus, Rev. 2:6, "This
thing I have, that I hate sin, and every sin as God hates it, and
because he hates it", as Christ owned them for this one grace, and
though they had many sins and many failings, yet, says he, this thou
hast etc. . . . If Christ will acknowledge thee to be his for one
earmark . . . thou mayest well plead it, even any one, to him.'[209]

(d) Trust not in anything else

On this point, Thomas Sharp, in his *Divine Comforts*, speaking of
Psalm 94:19, 'When the cares of my heart are many, thy consolations
cheer my soul', observes:

> The Psalmist was a man who discerned such an emptiness and
> insufficiency in all inferior contentments, as to seek no relief from
> them, nor take up with any of them as his rest in trouble; but in
> deepest anxiety and distress, did look for and find all his comfort
> solely in and from God. This is the very substance and marrow
> of the verse.[210]

Sharp applies the Psalmist's teaching roundly and forcefully, and
insists: 'Nothing can really comfort without God, or any further than
it leads to God. The creatures are but dry breasts and a mis-
carrying womb. The empty cisterns will sooner be filled with the
tears of the disappointed hopeless, than . . . replenish their souls
with the refreshing dews of true consolation. 'Tis in vain to look
for living comforts amongst dead enjoyments.'[211]

Moreover, with characteristic insight the Puritans insisted that
we are to refuse to trust, not only in carnal, but even in spiritual
things. Richard Sibbes writes to the purpose when he warns:

> And [as] for grace, though it be the beginning of a new creature
> in us, yet it is but the creature, and therefore not to be trusted in;
> nay, by trusting in it, we imbase [debase] it, and make it more
> imperfect. So far as there is truth of grace, it breeds distrust of
> ourselves, and carries the soul out of itself to the fountain of
> strength.[212]

Indeed, we dare not even trust in our trusting, insists Sibbes,
but only in 'God, whom it relies on, who is therefore called our
trust . . . God hath prescribed trust as the way to carry our souls

to himself, in whom we should only rely, and not in our imperfect trust, which hath its ebbing and flowing'.[213]

Perhaps a finer conclusion, and more complete summing-up of this point could not be found than is in the following paragraph, in which Thomas Goodwin acts as a mouthpiece for all the Puritan pastors in their dealings with deserted and troubled souls. Quoting Isaiah 50:10: 'Who among you fears the Lord, and obeys the voice of his servant; who walks in darkness and has no light, yet trusts in the name of the Lord, and relies upon his God?' Goodwin writes:

> The name of God alone, is here opposed to [distinguished from] all other means and props which faith has to rest on. It is opposed to all comfortable sense of God's love, to all sight of any grace in a man's self to which any promise is made. So that when a soul shall look into itself with one eye, and glance over all the Word of God with another; and yet shall see not any one grace in the one, nor promise in the other made to any grace within itself which it may rest upon; yet, the soul then looking upon God, and considering what a God he is, and what he says of himself, of his mercy and kindness and free grace towards sinful men; even the sole consideration of what merely it knows to be in God as he is revealed in the covenant of grace, may support him. This is to stay [rest trustfully] upon his name.[214]

Such counselling contains the very acme and genius of the Puritan pastoral theology.

(e) How to trust in this way

Here, the Puritan insistence upon right *method* in dealing with the life of the soul shows its true wisdom and potency; for most modern treatises on such a subject would inculcate trust as a matter of course, and might even define the idea closely, but few would tell the reader *how* to attain such trust, and tell it with that close practical instruction which marks the corresponding Puritan treatment. Here, a Cripplegate sermon-lecture by Matthew Sylvester entitled: *How may a gracious person from whom God hides his face, trust in the Lord as his God?*[215] admirably shows the pastoral skill of the Puritan methodology. It should perhaps be noted that here, as elsewhere, a 'gracious soul' is, in seventeenth century divinity, one that has received saving grace. Sylvester's 'directions' to such a soul are as follows:

> Direction I. *Let him retire into himself, and there compose his thoughts for close and serious work* (Ps. 4:4; 77:6); for here he will find a truly

great employment for every faculty and thought. . . . Here is
work within him and above him.   God and himself must now take
up his closest, deepest and most serious thoughts and pauses.
   Direction II.   *When thus retired and composed, let him discourse and
mind his gracious self.*   [Here, quoting appositely Eph. 2:10 and Isa.
26:12, as well as other texts, he concludes from them]: See what
wonders grace hath wrought already.   Hath God essayed to tear
thy soul out of Satan's paw?   Hath he transformed thy spirit, and
made it so much a resemblance of his own holiness and wisdom?
Hath he advanced thine esteem of holiness and heaven?   Hath he
cast out thy rubbish, and raised in thee a habitation for his own holy
name?   And will he demolish and disrespect a monument and
structure to his own praise?   Why did God thus illuminate thine
eyes, inflame thy heart with holy fervours, and so invigorate thy
active powers, as to enable thee to move toward him, but thou
mightest attain to and possess his highest favours and endearments.

Here, Sylvester inculcates an important maxim in the Puritan
writings: 'Grace is a principle and design so truly heavenly and
exalting as that its tendency proves its extraction, and manifests
God's purposes to do thee good for ever.'

   Direction III.   *Let them well observe how far the face of God is hid
from him indeed,*

lest he exaggerate, to his own and God's dishonour, the nature of
his state and the condition of grace within him.   Here Sylvester
quotes Isa. 49:14-16 and Ps. 77:6 and 10, and points out several
considerations by now familiar to the reader from this whole study,
to show the unchangeableness of God's love and the Christian's
standing in grace, and the always-limited nature of the Christian's
desertions.   Thus he continues:

   It is much to be observed, that God's dearest favourites have had
   the sharpest exercises and great darkness and disconsolateness on
   their spirits at some time or other.   For the sensible [felt] comforts
   and refreshments of religion are seldom found the daily fare of the
   exactest walkers with God under heaven.   And yet, how often are
   these eclipses greatened by their fancies or follies!   And then, by
   their misrepresentations of God to themselves, how oft and much is
   he dishonoured by them! . . .   Nay, I may boldly say it, that at the
   worst, more of God's face doth or may appear to them, and shine
   upon them, than is at any time hidden from them. . . .   And
   therefore it is a shameful thing, both to be pitied and blamed in
   gracious persons, that every intermission or retreat of sensible joys
   and favours, shall so enrage their fears and sorrows as that God's
   tenderness and faithfulness shall presently be arraigned, and his most
   gentle discipline heavily censured, strangely aggravated, extravagant-
   ly resented [intensely felt] and most immoderately bemoaned by
   them. . . .   Come then my soul, deal fairly with thyself and thy
   God, and tell me, What is it that God hath now denied thee?   How

I Gladly call to minde the time, when being yong, I heard, worthy Master PERKINS, so Preach in a great Assembly of Students, that he instructed them soundly in the Truth, stirred them up effectually to seeke after Godlinesse, made them fit for the kingdome of God; and by his owne example shewed them, what things they should chiefely intend, that they might promote true Religion, in the power of it, unto Gods glory, and others salvation:

And amongst other things which he Preached profitably, hee began at length to Teach, How with the tongue of the Learned one might speake a word in due season to him that is weary, out of *Esai.* 50.4. by untying and explaining diligently, *CASES OF CONSCIENCE* (as they are called.) And *the* LORD *found him so doing like a faithfull servant.* Yet left he many behinde him affected with that study; who by their godly Sermons (through Gods assistance) made it to runne, encrease, and be glorifyed throughout *England.*

My heart hath ever since been so set upon that Study, that I haue thought it worthy to be followed with all care, by all men. Since also (Gods good providence so disposing it) that I lived out of mine owne Countrey, I did obserue that in divers Churches, pure both for Doctrine and Order, this Practicall teaching was much wanting, and that this want was one of the chiefe causes of the great neglect, or carelesseneffe in some

A 3   duties

A famous preface. William Ames beginning his celebrated work on Conscience salutes the pioneer of this favourite Puritan study.

A formidable example of Puritan insight and Puritan industry, John Downame's huge folio 'The Christian Warfare' with its 2,000 columns of small print shows how seriously Puritanism regarded the spiritual warfare with sin and Satan. Downame knew more about his worst enemy than most know about their best friends!

THE
CASE AND CVRE
OF
A deserted Soule.
OR,
A TREATISE
Concerning the nature,
kinds, Degrees, Symptomes,
Causes, Cure of, and mistakes
about Spirituall Desertions.

BY
Ios: Symonds Minister of S^t. *Martins*
Iremonger Lane London.

I opened to my beloved, but my beloved had withdrawne
himselfe, and was gone; I sought him, but I could not find him;
I called him, but he gave me no answer. Cant. 5. 6.

Venit cum manifestatur, et cum occultatur abscedit, adest
tamen sive occultum, sive manifestum. *Aug. ep 3. p. 10.*

LONDON,
Printed by *T. Badger*, for *Luke Fawne*, at the Patriot in
Paul. Church yard. 1 6 4 1.

Behind this unassuming title-page lies just one of the many
treatises by long-forgotten (and never famous) Puritans which
ought to be ranked among the classics of religious literature.

*An ardent student of the Puritans, the author (featured above)
is convinced that their doctrine and example holds a timeless key
to prosperity for the Church in every generation.   A young minister
in a working class area of Nottingham, his growing and lively church
stands as a vivid argument for the timelessness of the Puritan gospel;
similarly his eloquent systematic expositions of Scripture claim
the contemporaneousness of the Puritan method.* (The publishers.)

far has God denied it? What of God is it that thou once hast seen,
but canst not now?

Direction IV. *Let him remove and shun all that provokes God thus to
hide his face.*[216]

After quoting Isa. 59:1,2 and the most pertinent Lam. 3:39,40,
our writer observes:

> No counsel nor encouragement will, or can, avail that soul for
> trust or conduct which neglects its stated work and watch, which
> God enjoins it to, and expects from it. . . . 'Repent and do your
> first works' was the grave and sober counsel (Rev. 2:5). Begin
> then, with thyself, and end with God, and work thyself up to his
> will, and thou shalt see his face with joy.[217]

Direction V. *Let him consider well how far God is unchangeably the
God of gracious souls.*

Here, Ps. 89:30-34, and Lev. 26:40,42-45, begin a sequence of
scriptural quotations which convince the author that:

> Pardoned sins, refined souls, accepted services, prayers and
> persons; with great victories, triumphs and salvations at the last;
> God's Spirit in them, his presence with them and his eternal glory
> for them when time is folded up and reckoned for: all these shall
> joyfully convince them in what respects and to what purpose God is
> immutably, and will be their God (Rom. 8:31-39).

Then, turning with wonderful wisdom as a pastor of souls to those
whose objections are understandably human, he continues:

> If parts [talents] be weak, if gifts be mean, if memory be frail
> through disadvantage of age or weakness; if passionate fervours be
> abated through those declensions which are entailed on mortals
> by a settled decree; must we infer from hence, that God hath hid his
> face from us, and holds us for his enemies unless he change the
> ordinary course of nature? . . . Must we from hence suspect or
> think that God disclaims us, and renounces all his merciful relations
> and regards to us? . . . God's covenant, and not your own thoughts
> or hopes must tell how far.[218]

Direction VI. *Let him consider and improve what God affords to help
and quicken trust in him.*

God, Sylvester assures us, has so ordered it, in his wisdom, that
he 'hath his part, and man hath his to do'. 'Trust,' he continues,
'is a compounded act of duty, made up of assent, consent and
reliance; and it respects veracity, goodness and fidelity in the object
trusted in,' but on the part of the subject who is trusting,

> God . . . expects that gracious souls shall fix their deepest thoughts
> upon what he hath given them to fix and raise their trust upon.
> Idleness doeth no good . . . he that expects [that] God should
> miraculously inspire trust into him without that intervenient use
> of his own faculties in the improvement of those helps which God

affords, will find such hopes and trust fitter to be rebuked and frustrated, than to be gratified and fulfilled.[219]

It is salutary here, to notice how such counsel steers its way between a dangerous mysticism (reflected in the last quotation) on the one hand, and a hectic and fruitless activism on the other. A lasting peace of mind, like every other ingredient and product of true spirituality, resulted, in Puritan thought, from a right 'consideration' of God and a true 'improvement' of that knowledge in devotion and service.

After the counsel 'fly to God' and 'trust in God', a further main direction to troubled Christians was:

(iii) Put convictions of sin into perspective

As in most spiritual depressions, conviction due to sin in general or sins (real or imagined) in particular, plays a large part; the Puritan physician of the soul spent valuable time instructing Christians in the true sorrow for sin, and gently steering them from the extremes of 'overmuch sorrow' on the one hand, and 'antinomian presumption' on the other. Christopher Love has written largely and frequently on this matter, and he will act as chief spokesman for the Puritan pastors in his teaching on this point.

(a) The occasions when there is too much sorrow for sin

As there may be too little sorrow for sin, so, in a well-meaning but mistaken soul, there may be too much sorrow. The soul's sorrow for sin may itself become, by its extremes, sin, for, observes William Bridge in this connection, 'discouragement is itself a sin: a gospel sin. My sin against law is no just cause why I should sin against the gospel'.[220] Christopher Love lists nine cases in which the soul is excessively cast down because of its sin, not moderating grief with proper comforts:

> First, a man is cast down too much for sin, when his humiliation maketh him to cast off all hopes of pardon . . . the saints on earth are to carry their hopes still above all discouragements, and to hope strongly for pardon of sin: better have the thread of our lives cut off than the anchor-chord of our hope: despair is the cutting off of hope. But to be cast down under sin as to have despairing thoughts, without hope of mercy, is excessive.
> But secondly: that man is cast down for sin too much, when he

is so cast down that he doth cast off duty: when a man shall thus reason against himself: 'What need I pray? and what need I perform holy duties? I know God will not hear me. . . . And what need I hear sermons, I know God will not hear me, nor accept of my duties; and I shall not get good by all that I do, and by all that I hear.' These reasonings, O man, are very sinful, and it argues a great degree of too much humiliation for sin.

Thirdly: thy casting down for sin is too much, when thou art so dejected and cast down for sin that it doth indispose thee for holy duties. . . . Composedness of spirit aright for humiliation of sin, is so far from unfitting the soul for duty and prayer, that it doth dispose and fit the soul for prayer to God (Hos. 12:4; Jer. 3:21; Neh. 9:1,4). . . . When thy sight of sin, and the sense of sin, and humiliation for sin doth fill thy heart with matter fit for prayer, that is necessary and good: but when by this the soul is unfitted for prayer and supplication, then it is sinful.

Fourthly: then a man is too much cast down for sin, when there is an unaptness, unwillingness in the mind to receive and apply comfortable [strengthening] counsels that are laid down in the word, and which do appertain to him in that condition. . . . When God shall call to thee and say, 'come to me all ye that are weary and heavy laden, and I will ease you', Matt. 11:28, and you refuse and put off comfort from you, you are too much cast down for sin.[221]

Love's fifth point reveals much practical commonsense. The Puritans were not ascetics and while fasting and self-denial had its place in Puritan practice, Love can still write:

Fifthly: then is a man cast down too much for sin under the weight and sense and sight of sin, when that sorrow for sin shall be an occasion to wrong and hurt and to disturb the body by diseases. . . . The Lord hath bid thee mourn, not to rack and crucify thy body but thy lusts; he calls thee to weep out thy sin's strength and life, not thy body's strength and life.[222]

Elsewhere in the same treatise he returns to this point quoting the text in Isa. 61:8: 'I hate robbery for a burnt offering' and comments: 'So . . . it is not God's sacrifice that is prejudicial to bodily health;'[223] and suggests that Heman and Asaph and David were not without fault in this matter (eg. Ps. 88;77; 31:9,10; 42:4).[224]

Love continues with typical Puritan sagacity:

Sixthly: men are then cast down for sin too much, when a man is so far and so much cast down under the sight and sense of sin that he hath no mind at all to follow his particular calling. Now this is sinful sorrow . . . and the reason is this, as all divines say, that God doth never require any duty which belongs to our general calling as Christians to be inconsistent with our particular callings as men.

'And herein' he adds later, 'the devil's policy lies: that if he in trouble of mind can keep a man out of his calling, he hath the better way to work upon an idle man.'

Seventhly: they are too much cast down for sin when the amiable and admirable and comforting attributes of God are formidable and terrible to such men; when we think of sin as not to think on the divine attributes of God: of the mercy of God, of the goodness of God, of the patience of God, of the longsuffering of God, of the faithfulness of God; when men shall think so of God as if he were all justice, all wrath without mercy.   Good men have been overtaken with this fault, Job was so, Job 23:15: 'Therefore am I troubled at his presence: when I consider, I am afraid of him. . . .'   And this was Asaph's case: 'I remembered God and I was troubled. . . .'   Oh but the thoughts of God comforted David's soul: 'When I thought on thy name, I was comforted' (saith holy David) Ps. 94:19.   Aye, but said Asaph, 'when I thought on God I was troubled'; and Job, 'when I thought on God, on the Almighty, I was afraid of him'. When the attributes of God shall trouble men to think of them, and not encourage them and comfort them, then is this sorrow too much casting down for sin.

But then, eighthly: when under this sorrow for sin thou canst not look to God and bless God for common mercies and special grace, (God gives thee mercies, great mercies that thou mayest be rich, and follows thee with mercies and blessings and loving kindnesses daily), . . . and yet for all this, [for] God not to have glory from thee, shows thou art too much cast down for sin. . . .   When God gives thee grace, to assist thee against manifold temptations, and to keep thee from the committing of manifold sins, and to help thee against thy corruptions, and to give thee grace to establish thy heart—and yet not to bring up thy heart under thy sorrows to bless God: there is a sinful sorrow.[225]

Our author here illustrates his point with a memorable analogy:

If a man be upon his knees, he may see heaven above and earth beneath: but for a man to lie flat upon his face, he cannot see either the heaven above nor any creature; but only the earth below him. So, when God brings thee to thy knees for sin, then you can see a gracious God, a faithful God, a merciful God, a pitiful Father; and then you can see those blessings that God bestoweth upon you, and bless and glorify God.   But when you throw yourself on the ground by a faithful sorrow, and lie on your faces for sin to be too much humbled under the sight and sense of it: in this case God hath neither glory, nor you comfort.[226]

Christopher Love gives as his last example of over-much grief for sin, what is, perhaps, his chief instance:

But ninthly, when your sins do discourage your souls from laying hold on Jesus Christ, then thou art cast down too much for sin: that man is surely sick to death when his disease will not let him send for a physician . . . whereas true sorrow and gospel humiliation for sin . . . is such a measure and degree of sorrow, that instead of discouraging the soul to go away from Christ, it doth encourage the soul to come to Christ, and to lay hold on Christ, and to prize Jesus

Christ above all in the world. But that is a sinful sorrow when it drives the soul off from Christ, and discourageth the soul from coming to him, and from setting a high estimation and price upon him.[227]

Love concludes his teaching on this whole matter, in a pungent sentence towards the end of his treatise. 'What is the end [purpose] of trouble of mind for sin?' he asks; and answers: 'The end is to embitter sin, and to provoke a soul to look out after Jesus Christ.'[228]

(b) The reasons why there is sometimes too much sorrow for sin

Here, Love answers briefly and succinctly in five reasons:

A first reason is this: it ariseth partly from that softness of heart, and that tenderness of conscience that is implanted in God's people by God. The eye is troubled at a mote when the hand is not troubled at a greater thing; the eye is the tenderest part of the body. Why, beloved, God's people have tender consciences, sin on their consciences is as a mote in their eye that greatly troubles them.

A second cause or reason is this: God's people are troubled for sin because God's people, seeing themselves that they are more in sinning against God than they are obeying God, sin troubles and disquiets them the more: grace is as the gleanings of the vintage, and sin is as the full harvest . . . God's people see their sins like mountains and their graces like molehills.

A third reason is this: because sin is more visible and manifest to the soul than their graces are, therefore they are more troubled for sin . . . a man may more easily discern and have a sight of his sin than a godly man can have sight of his grace.

A fourth reason is drawn from a consideration that Christ's soul was troubled for sin . . . and this makes the godly man reflect: 'Shall Christ's soul be troubled for my sin that was imputed to him, and shall not I be troubled for sin that is inherent in me?

A fifth reason is this: that the people of God might taste and see the evil and bitterness of sin the more in the course of their lives, and may be more put in awe to commit sin for the time to come.[229]

(c) Rules for restoring a right and balanced condition

To souls thus cast down, Love has not only a right diagnosis of their trouble, but the right cure for it also. His rules for restoring a Christian who is too depressed by conviction of sin are eight in number, and again he is the representative here, as elsewhere, of the typical Puritan method and matter of pastoral theology.

First: when thou art excessively troubled under the guilt of sin, take this rule: what troubled thoughts thou hast about the guilt of sin, spend them upon the *power* of sin within thee; this is a holy diversion—to be always conversant about the power of sin; it is an evangelical and precious temper. If Christians were more troubled about the power of sin, they would be less troubled about the guilt of sin; the Devil doth not care if professors of religion be terrified Christians, so they be not mortified Christians.

Secondly: keep conscience clear, that thou do not add guilt to guilt. Adding guilt to guilt is the way to add horror to horror and terror to terror upon the conscience . . . to have a conscience pacified which is not purified is but to skin over an old sore, which before it be healed will break out again. 'Peace,' saith Bernard, 'in many men is worse than spiritual conflict.'

A third rule is this: take heed thou dost not go about to allay the disquiet of thy soul for sin by sin . . . to run to vain pleasures and to sensual delight . . . it is just as [if] a man that is athirst . . . will drink a draught of poison to quench his thirst!

A fourth rule is this: fix your eyes on the evidences of your graces when your hearts are overmuch disquieted in the sight of sin. As trouble of conscience in the sight of his grace; so the evidence or sight of grace will keep a man that he shall not be excessively troubled in the sight of his sin.

Fifthly: ponder in your meditations the comfortable [strengthening] promises of the gospel rather than the threats of the Law. If I were to speak to a secure sinner, I would give him a quite contrary rule: that he should rather ponder on the threats of the Law than on the promises of the gospel. But to a sinner greatly pressed under the weight of God's wrath, he must take this word rather to ponder on—the promising part of the word than on the threatening part of the word.

A sixth rule: compare the guilt of your sins with the merits of Christ's righteousness, and you will find that there is more in Christ's righteousness to save than is in sin to damn. Christ's righteousness is imputed to a believer that the guilt of sin might not be charged on him. As Christ's person is above thy person, so Christ's righteousness is above thy righteousness; this the apostle layeth down, Rom. 5:15, 'The gift by grace hath abounded to many'. The gift doth exceed the sin, exceed the offence; compare but them in thy thoughts and that will be a means to allay the trouble of thy heart.

Seventhly: disclose and reveal that sin, the guilt whereof doth so much disquiet thy soul, unto some judicious, compassionate and experienced Christian; giving vent to your own sorrows by complaints is a great way to ease the mind. If in innocency God thought fit that Adam should not be left alone, but should have a helper, much more now, in a state of dejection, since the fall, do we need others' help as well as our own. If Jesus Christ, when in an agony, God thought fit to send an angel to comfort him; O then, do not believers need much more when they are in their spiritual agony and conflicts and temptations . . . some to comfort them? The apostle on this ground bids Christians to comfort one another, 1 Thess. 4:18, 'Comfort you one another' etc.; 1 Thess. 5:14, 'Comfort the feeble minded, support the weak, be patient toward all men'. God doth enjoin Christians to this mutual act of love: comfort ye one another: as it is [with] an arch, it is so artificially built that though the stones of an arch do all hang downwards, yet one stone doth support another that they do not fall. O beloved Christians, that are lively stones in Christ's spiritual building, you should be as stones of an arch, that though one stone doth hang downward, yet the stones next to it should bear it up. This makes Solomon say two is better than one, for if one fall, the other should help him up.

The eighth rule is this: when thou art disquieted for sin, then go to God through Christ in prayer to pacify thy conscience and speak peace to thy soul when thou art troubled. We can speak peace, but it is God that gives peace: this is one prerogative ascribed to God, that he be a God that comforts them that are cast down, 2 Cor. 7:6: 'Nevertheless, God that comforteth those that are cast down, comforted us by the coming of Titus.' He is a God that creates peace out of nothing. It is very observable in Isa. 8:11: 'For the Lord spake this to me with a strong hand, and instructed me that I should not walk in the way of this people,' that when God would comfort the prophets against the accusations and combinations of the enemies against the Church of God, he spake to them with a strong hand. The tongue is the instrument of speech, not the hand; we speak with our tongues, we can speak to a man comfortable words, but we cannot make you believe them; but the Scripture saith God speaks with his hand, because he can do what he speaks. His word is like Christ's word in the ninth chapter of Mark: Christ spoke to the winds, and lo, they were still, and there was a great calm. Beloved, God's word hath a hand in it, it can do what it speaks: 'O then, go to God through Christ in prayer. And in having recourse to God, there are two things you are to beg of God in prayer if you would have the trouble of soul allayed. First, beg of God to have a share in the blood of Christ that merits thy peace; and to have a share in the Spirit of Christ that works thy peace. These are the two main things in prayer to allay the trouble of soul for the guilt of sin.[230]

After some further points of comfort supplementary to these 'rules', our author handsomely concludes:

Take this for thy comfort, that there are more promises of the gospel made to men in this condition than to any other sort of men in the world. I could give you multitudes of promises to men in this case: Matt. 11:28, 'Come unto me all ye that labour and are heavy laden, and I will give you rest'. So, in Isa. 54:10,11; 35:4; 57:15. Many other texts I could give you where God maketh abundant promises to men under disquiet of soul, under the guilt of sin. When children are well, they shall have, it may be, but pebble stones to play withal. But if there be one sick child in the house, the mother goes to the cabinet and looketh out fine things to quiet the child. O beloved, it may be [that] healthful Christians shall go on com-

fortably, and shall have now and then smiles of God's face toward
them; but God's rich cabinet of promises are open to them when
they are sick.   When a poor sinner suspects that he is not pardoned:
then God comes with a promise to comfort him that he is pardoned.
The well child in the house is beloved by the parents, but the sick
child is dandled on the knees; the well child may have bread and
butter, but the sick child hath comfortable things to comfort it.
Beloved, God's sick children, that are sick with sin, that are greatly
troubled in conscience, God provides for them the promises to allay
and pacify the troubled spirit.   O let words of comfort sink into your
hearts.[231]

(d) Directions for preventing an unbalanced conviction of sin

Christopher Love lays down three such directions:
   'The first rule is: do not expect so much sorrow and casting down
as some other men have had . . . it may be thou canst not bear
that which other men can: that ballast [which] will but serve a
ship would overload a little boat . . . God in his wisdom sees some
men that they stand in need . . . of a greater measure of affliction
and casting down for sin than others have need of.'
   'The second rule is this: rest satisfied in thy conscience, though
thou mayest not find the measure of thy humiliation, yet if thou
find the *end* of thy humiliation rest satisfied in that.   If in thy
humiliation thou dost desire to be truly humbled for sin; and if
thou dost desire to lay thyself low in the presence of God; if thou
dost desire to abhor thyself in regard of the sinfulness of thy nature
and life; and if thou dost desire to amend thy ways and thy doings
that have not been good: if so, though thou hast not the measure of
humiliation and casting down for sin as others have, yet thou hast
the end of humiliation and thou mayest rest satisfied in thy conscience.   If that humiliation doth embitter sin, and endear Jesus
Christ in thy soul, I tell thee O poor soul, . . . thou mayest be dear
to Jesus Christ, . . . and I tell thee further for thy comfort, there
was never yet any went to hell for want of degrees of grace: but
many go to hell and lose heaven for want of truth of grace.   So,
none ever went to hell for want of such-and-such a degree of . . .
humiliation: but many go to hell for want of humiliation in the least
measure and truth of it.'
   'The third rule . . . is this: be sure to cast thyself upon Jesus
Christ for life and salvation, and then whatever comes, be sure thou
wilt not be too much cast down for sin, nor too much dejected under

it. What is the great reason that so many poor souls are so much cast down for sin, too much dejected under the sight and sense of it? It is this: because they are afraid to cast themselves wholly upon Jesus Christ, and to roll themselves upon him for salvation. Though more sin requires more tears upon the thoughts of it, yet Jesus Christ need not shed more blood for sin; Jesus Christ needs no more to die for the satisfaction for sin; Christ hath paid a full and complete and sufficient ransom for sin, and needs die no more.'[232]

One of the greatest theologians of the Puritan movement, John Owen, provides a summing up of much of Love's teaching in a passage which finely combines acuteness of thought with true pastoral feeling:

> Some, finding the weight and burden of their sins, and being called to mourning and humiliation on that account, are so taken up with it as to lose the sense of forgiveness which, rightly improved, would promote their sorrow as their sorrow seems directly to sweeten their sense of forgiveness. Sorrow absolutely exclusive of the faith of forgiveness, is legal and tendeth unto death; and not a persuasive from him that calleth us: but gospel sorrow and gospel assurance may well dwell in the same breast at the same time . . . I am persuaded that generally, they mourn most who have most assurance. And all true gospel mourners will be found to have the root of assurance so grafted in them, that in its proper season – a time of trouble – it will undoubtedly flourish.[233]

The fourth major direction we shall give from the Puritan writings aiming at a cure of spiritual depression is:

(iv) Do your part in all this

The immediate comforts and consolations of the Holy Spirit are not at the command of the Christian; but the power and encouragement of the Spirit working by the Word are ever at the believer's disposal. For this reason the Puritan pastors were able to remind the most depressed and discouraged soul that a way was still open to him, even in the worst times, which was itself glorious and God-glorifying. Says Richard Sibbes to the believer in such conflict: 'Every work of a Christian is beautiful in its own time. The graces of Christianity have their several offices at several seasons.' Even times of desertion and depression provide the regenerate soul with its own opportunities of glorifying God, for, says Sibbes, 'Praising God in this life hath this prerogative, that here we praise him "in the midst of his enemies" Ps. 110:2'.[234] The same writer, quoting

David's words in Ps. 42:11 – 'I shall yet praise him' – even maintains that this act of praising God in sorrow and lethargy of soul, is itself the first part of deliverance from that condition:

> He mentioneth here praising God, instead of deliverance, because a heart enlarged to praise God is indeed the greatest part of the deliverance; for by it the soul is delivered out of its own straits and discontent.[235]

From this, it follows that a first direction given to such a Christian in such circumstances would generally be:

(a) Seek to praise and please God more than to be delivered from depression and desertion

Christopher Love is sure that desertions are often experienced and prolonged because Christians 'Do look more after comfort than they do after grace; and this is the cause why they want [lack] more comfort than they need to want; they look more after marks and signs that may tell them what they are, than after precepts which tell them what they should do. When Christians shall be enquiring after privileges more than . . . their duty, it is just with God to keep their comfort from them'.[236]

Robert Asty, in his little classic *Rejoicing in the Lord Jesus in all cases and conditions*, gives, in one chapter, some 'Earnest directions to a believer whilst in the dark concerning his interest [share] in Christ Jesus'.[237] At one point he writes: 'Prefer service for Christ before assurance in Christ, and esteem duty for and towards Christ, before consolation in Christ,' and adds:

> It argues a very low and mercenary spirit to act only for or towards the Lord upon the feelings of our interest in him, or only for the comforts that do attend a sensible [felt] interest in him. No, we must follow Christ wherever he goeth, and prefer service for Christ before comfort in Christ; and resolve to follow Christ, and to serve him whether he do settle us and comfort us or not . . . so the believer . . . should prefer a command before a promise, and assistance for duty before incomes in a duty.[238]

Samuel Rutherford sees a notable example of this in the Syrophenician woman of the gospels who seemed to be cast off by Christ, and yet: 'She putteth Christ in his chair of state, and adoreth him. The deserted soul saith: be what I will, he is Jehovah the Lord.'[239]

(b) Praise him for what he has done in the past

Thomas Goodwin writes on this point: 'The remembrance of former things doth often uphold, when present sense [feeling] fails. This Asaph practised in a like case, Psalm 77 . . . and so Job did, when he was thus stricken and forsaken of God: he views over every part of his life, he seeks what dry land he could find to get a footing upon in the midst of seas of temptations . . . chapters 29, 30 and chapter 31.'[240] This maxim Goodwin goes on to apply in typical Puritan strain:

> And canst thou call nothing to remembrance betwixt God and thee which argues infallibly his love? What! Nothing? Look again. Did God never speak peace unto thy heart and shed his love abroad in it? Hast thou at no time found in thine heart pure strains of true love and goodwill to him; some pure drops of godly sorrow for offending him, and found some dispositions of pure self-denial wherein thou didst simply aim at his glory more than thine own good?[241]

Such questions to a Christian soul have within themselves their own answer, and Goodwin is therefore able to conclude:

> These things you are to recall and consider in time of distress: to remember former graces and spiritual dispositions in you, and God's gracious dealings with you. God remembers them to have mercy on you, and why should not you remember them to comfort you? Therefore, Heb. 6:9,10, 'We hope' says he 'better things of you, for God is not unrighteous to forget your labour of love', namely to reward you. And therefore he calls upon them in like manner, Heb. 10:32, 'to call to remembrance the former days' to comfort them; how they held out when their hearts were tried to the bottom; when shipwreck was made of their goods, good names, and all for Christ – yet they made not shipwreck of a good conscience.[242]

It is worthwhile inserting Robert Asty's note on this matter. He writes: 'Upon the rising of new darkness, have recourse unto the former experiences that thou hast had of peace, joy and comfort in believing. God, it may be, doth withhold a new Word because he would have thee go to the old Word that he hath spoken before; and God may withhold a new sign because he would have thee go to the old sign that he gave thee for a discovery before.'[243]

(c) Do your first works

But such is the power of depression and the craft of Satan in the Christian soul, that often all former mercies and graces are put in

doubt and their genuineness becomes a matter of dispute. The
Christian is then forced to take the following recourse on which
Thomas Goodwin has written with great wisdom:

> Renew thy faith and repentance, set thy heart a-work to believe
> and repent afresh as if thou hadst never yet begun. . . . And to
> that end make this use of whatsoever flaws the devil finds in either
> – to direct thee what to mend and rectify for time to come . . . and
> this direction I now prescribe to you because in time of temptation
> about assurance it is the usual course of some troubled souls to spend
> all their thoughts about what formerly they have had, as if they
> must have comfort only from the former work or no way.[244]

Goodwin admits that at first glance this would seem contrary to
his previous direction – that the soul without present assurance and
comfort should derive it from the consideration of past and happier
spiritual experiences – but points out that this direction is really
complementary to the former, for: 'You are not only to take that
course, nor to look back so much to your former faith and repentance as to forget to practice new [that is renew your faith and
repentance] and the truth is in the end you must come back to this
[renewal]; for God's great end in deserting is to put you upon
renewing your faith and repentance.'[245]

Moreover, this complementary course will certainly add, in time,
to the significance and force of past experiences; for our author
continues: 'And whereas thou thinkest that by this thou mayest
prejudice thy former title, that is not my meaning as if thou shouldst
utterly give up thy old faith and repentance as counterfeit . . . only
my advice is to forbear, and to cease pleading of it for a time, and
to begin to renew it rather. . . . And then the comfort of thy old
repentance will come in. As the apostle says of the law, so I of thy
former title "it is not destroyed, but established" rather by this.'[246]
William Bridge provides a very clear and winsome example of how
this may be done when he writes:

> Look what you would do if you were seeking to be justified, and
> do the same now. If I were seeking to be justified, having a sight
> of my own sin and nature, I would, through grace, come to the
> righteousness of Christ, and rest the weight of my poor, guilty soul
> upon it. . . . And as faith justifies and gives peace at first, so the
> renewing of this act of faith renews our peace. And what is my
> justifying faith but in time of temptation to rest myself and condition
> upon Christ alone, saying: 'Whether godly or ungodly, whether in
> Christ or not in Christ, now I do not dispute, but rest myself upon
> Christ alone.' This do again and this will bring peace again.[247]

(d) When you cannot do what you would – do what you can

'God,' says William Bridge, 'will receive a little when you are much discouraged;'[248] but that 'little', Joseph Symonds insists, is truly ours to give even as it is God's to command, and it is within our power to give that 'little' even at the worst times of spiritual depression:

> You must set your hands to the work; for it is in vain to expect that God should help you if you will not help yourselves. . . . Remember what I have said: you have a life in you if you be in Christ, and as you have a life, so there is a never-failing presence of the Holy Spirit to attend that power which you have. . . . It is certain a godly man cannot by the strength of his endeavours *alone* raise up his soul, nor recover his loss . . . but the strength of all our endeavours is the grace and promise of God; but as endeavours without God cannot, so God without endeavours will not.[249]

Besides the many directions found throughout this section on the cure of spiritual depressions, there remain two main things which the depressed Christian can and should do even in the lowest condition of soul. First of all, the discouraged believer was told, you can attend upon the means of grace – the ordinances of God. This, it was often said, is the 'waiting posture' that the saints can and must take up in such times. Thomas Goodwin counsels: 'Wait upon God, thus trusting in his name, in the constant use of all the ordinances and means of comfort. Waiting is indeed but an act of faith further stretched out.'[250] Nor is this waiting the act of faith at its lowest and of doubtful quality; rather it is faith in one of its most vital and victorious activities. As Goodwin writes:

> Waiting is an act of faith resting on God; an act of hope expecting from him; an act of patience, the mind quietly contenting itself 'till God doth come; and of submission if he should not come. Therefore, says the Church, being in the very case, Lam. 3:26, 'It is good to hope and quietly to wait for the salvation of the Lord'.[251]

However, it must be noted that this 'waiting' is not at all a mystic inertia; it is patience in activity not in lethargy, and Goodwin enforces his counsel by adding: 'And waiting thus, go on to use all the means of grace more diligently, more constantly though thou findest a long while no good by them.'[252] This realistic quotation was founded upon an essential and oft-repeated principle which Goodwin is careful to inculcate: 'That trouble of mind doth only [alone] hurt you that drives you away from the means,' for such a resort would add sin to sorrow, and make culpable that state which before might have been without blame. 'Therefore,' observes Goodwin, 'the Devil endeavours nothing more than to keep such souls from the word, from good company, from the sacraments, from prayer by objecting their unprofitableness unto them, and that all is in vain, and that you do but increase your condemnation.'[253]

At this point a warning from Robert Asty is apposite; for it is important to realise that the 'waiting upon God' is not to be in expectation of a marvellous and dramatic experience, for this is not to be looked for. Asty thus writes:

> Diligently attend all discovering [revealing] ordinances, but bound [limit] your desires after a sense of interest [a feeling that you have a share in Christ] in waiting upon the Lord in the ways that he hath consecrated for the dispensing of it. . . . Do not think that there must be a voice from heaven to settle you and satisfy you; do not look for some miraculous . . . impressions upon you, but bound your desires after the sense of your interest in his own way. And that which makes me mention it is this: that Satan forces many souls upon this; they cannot believe an ordinary evidence, and a small sign will not serve them; but they must have some immediate appearance from heaven, an immediate testimony from heaven in some miraculous way upon their spirits or else they cannot think that their state is good. And the design of Satan here, is to drive you into such a way wherein you shall certainly meet with a disappointment, and being under a disappointment, then you may more easily and more strongly question your state. But we are not to expect revelations nor miraculous operations, but to wait upon the Lord in his own consecrated ways that he hath appointed for the dispensing of pardon, of peace, and comfort and the evidence of our interest.[254]

One particular ordinance of value at times of desertion, it was suggested, is the reading and hearing of the Word of God, and Jeremiah Burroughs as well as Thomas Goodwin mentions it particularly. Burroughs writes appositely: 'If thou canst not see God's face, yet hearken and see if thou canst hear his voice and follow that . . . and follow his voice though it be in the dark. . . . Perhaps the Word is not a comforting Word to thee as heretofore, aye, but is it not a directing Word, an instructing Word, an enlightening Word? Oh this now should support thee for the present.'[255]

Burroughs concludes, therefore, 'Oh then, keep to the path where thou wert wont to meet with God, for thou shalt meet with him again'.[256]

The other thing which, it was said, the believer, even in desertion can and must do is to *reason with himself*, guided and preserved in this by the Word and the Spirit. Very much of the foregoing work counsels reflection upon the character and promises of God, the

nature of faith and the covenant of grace, and it is very significant
that the Puritan pastors laid much stress upon mental acts as being
of vital practical use to the Christian.   Indeed there are perhaps
few things more significant in Puritan practical divinity than the
place given to the power of right spiritual thinking in various situations.   The very term 'practical divinity', far from being a term to
cover the work of the body only, was used among them to include
the acts and operations either receptive or active, of the whole man;
and it was considered that directions to the mind and heart were as
truly 'practical' as instructions regarding purely physical behaviour.
Thus the constantly-appearing terms 'meditate', 'consider' and
'reflect' were, to all the Puritan writers and pastors, terms belonging
to the vital and noble activity of the Christian, and as really practical
as the work of hand or foot.

As the evidence of this is scattered throughout what has already
been written, it will be necessary only to forward two comprehensive
and conclusive quotations to show the force and significance of such
'reasoning' with oneself.

Joseph Symonds, directing his words to the depressed soul at this
point, affirms:

> God hath made the understanding the guide and treasure of the
> soul: upon this altar lieth the fire of God; if these coals be blowed up
> and cast upon the heart, they will warm, melt, purge and quicken
> it.[257] [In demonstration and proof of this principle he continues]:
> There are two things in a renewed mind: (i) A treasure of habitual
> knowledge: it is as the ark of God in which the tables of the law are
> kept; the mystery of the gospel is engraven on it. . . .   (ii) There is a
> power to use and improve these truths by meditation and application
> . . . the understanding is to the heart as the breast to the child, or
> as the stomach to the body – all is fed by it.[258].

Richard Sibbes concludes from similar reasoning: 'By this means
we shall never want [lack] a divine to comfort us, a physician to
cure us, a counsellor to direct us, a musician to cheer us, a controller
to check us, because, by the help of the Word and Spirit, we can be
all these to ourselves.'[259]

CONCLUSION

In all that has gone before, the Puritans' pastoral genius is amply demonstrated, and in a day of easy censure of the 'deserted' as having some notable sin in their life, or as culpably failing 'to claim the victory', we do well to hear the Puritan pastor counselling this frequently experienced and as frequently misunderstood state. Every Christian is aware of the many forms of spiritual depression that can and do accompany the Christian life in this uncertain world. Perhaps few ages have been more neurotic than our own, and the crying need for an adequate, biblical, pastoral ministry to anguished minds, disillusioned Christians, stricken consciences and subconscious fears, was never more in evidence than in our day.

Such cases, and in such number, need more studied and scriptural treatment than they are receiving. Bad surgery can cure a corn and cause a cancer! Ill-considered advice can bring immeasurable harm to troubled souls, sooner or later. In this matter, as in all others, we have the Puritans' Bible, the Puritans' God – why may we not have 'the Puritans' genius'?

REFERENCES

PART ONE   THE PURITAN IN THE PULPIT

[1] *The Works of Henry Smith*, 2 vols. Nichol edition, 1866, vol 1, p. 134.
[2] John Mayer, *Praxis Theologica: or The Epistle of the Apostle St. James* . . . *Expounded*, 1629 (ch. 5, p. 127).
[3] See *The Complete Works of Thomas Brooks*, 6 vols. Nichol edition, 1866-7, vol. 1, p. xxvii.
[4] *The Whole Works of the Right Rev. Edward Reynolds, D.D.*, 6 vols. Ed. Pitman, 1826, vol. 5, p. 343.
[5] Arthur Hildersham, *CLII Lectures upon Psalm LI*, folio, 1642, p. 732.
[6] Paul Bayne, *A Commentary upon Ephesians*, folio, 1658, p. 246.
[7] *The Complete Works of Richard Sibbes, D.D.*, 6 vols. Nichol edition, 1862-4, vol. 5, p. 509.
[8] Nehemiah Rogers, *The True Convert*, 1632, part 2, pp. 73-4.
[9] *The Works of that famous and worthy minister of Christ in the University of Cambridge, Mr. William Perkins*, 1618, 3 vols., vol. 3, p. 445.
[10] *Select Practical Writings of Robert Traill*, Edinburgh, 1845, p. 120.
[11] Perkins, *op. cit.*, p. 445.
[12] *A Practical and Polemical Commentary* . . . *upon The Third and Fourth Chapters of the Latter Epistle of St. Paul to Timothy*, folio, 1658, p. 329.
[13] Reynolds, *op. cit.*, vol. 5, pp. 344-5.
[14] Traill, *op. cit.*, p. 126.
[15] John Downame, *The Christian Warfare*, 4th edition, 1634, p. 158.
[16] Mayer, *op. cit.*, ch. 1, p. 182.
[17] *The Morning Exercises at Cripplegate*, 6 vols. Nichol edition, 1844-5, vol. 5, p. 278.
[18] *The Works of that Faithful and Painful Preacher, Mr. Elnathan Parr*, folio, 1633, Rom. 10:14 ad loc.
[19] *The Works of Thomas Goodwin, D.D.*, 12 vols. Nichol edition, 1861-66, vol. 11, pp. 360-1.
[20] *ibid.*, pp. 361-4.
[21] Mayer, *op. cit.*, ch. 1, p. 183.
[22] N. Rogers, *op. cit.*, p. 12.
[23] Richard Rogers, *Seven Treatises*, folio, 1603, pp. 214-5.
[24] Sibbes, *op. cit.*, p. 508.
[25] Arthur Hildersham, *op. cit.*, pp. 733-4.
[26] *The Works of John Owen*, Goold edition, Exposition of Hebrews, vol. 4, p. 245, ad loc. Heb. 4: 1, 2.
[27] Goodwin, *op. cit.*, p. 364.
[28] N. Rogers, *op. cit.*, p. 71.
[29] Nicholas Byfield, *An Exposition upon the Epistle to the Colossians*, 4th edition, folio, 1649, ch. 1, pp. 49-50.
[30] *The Works of John Flavel*, 6 vols., Banner of Truth reprint, 1968, vol. 6, p. 568.
[31] Richard Baxter, *Gildas Silvianus; The Reformed Pastor*, 2nd edition, 1657, pp. 14-25.
[32] *ibid.*, pp. 25-47.
[33] *ibid.*, p. 19.
[34] William Attersol, *A Commentary upon the Epistle of Saint Paul to Philemon*, 2nd edition, folio, 1633, p. 34.
[35] *op. cit.*, p. 569.
[36] *ibid.*, p. 572.
[37] *op. cit.*, p. 123.
[38] Owen, *Works*, vol. 15, p. 118.
[39] *The Complete Works of Thomas Manton*, Nisbet edition, 22 vols., 1870-1875, vol. 4, p. 153.
[40] James Durham, *A Commentary upon The Book of the Revelation*, quarto, Glasgow, 1680, p. 228.
[41] *ibid.*, p. 224.
[42] Sibbes, *op. cit.*, pp. 505-6.

PART TWO   THE PURITAN IN THE PEW

[1] John Wells, *The Practical Sabbatarian: or Sabbath Holiness Crowned with Superlative Happiness*, London, 1668, p. 274.
[2] Jeremiah Burroughs, *Gospel Worship*, 1648, p. 164.
[3] *ibid.*, p. 166.
[4] *Cripplegate Exercises*, vol. 4, p. 181.
[5] Burroughs, *op. cit.*, p. 166.
[6] *ibid.*, p. 164.
[7] *ibid.*, p. 167.
[8] *ibid.*, p. 171.
[9] *ibid.*, p. 171.
[10] *ibid.*, pp. 171-2.
[11] Wells, *op. cit.*, p. 279.
[12] *Cripplegate Exercises*, vol. 4, p. 182.
[13] Burroughs, *op. cit.*, p. 175.
[14] Wells, *op. cit.*, p. 301.
[15] *ibid.*, p. 312.
[16] Burroughs, *op. cit.*, p. 175.
[17] *ibid.*, p. 176.
[18] *The Works of George Swinnock, M.A.*, 5 vols, Nichol edition, 1868, vol. 1, p. 161.
[19] *ibid.*, p. 162.
[20] Burroughs, *op. cit.*, p. 177.
[21] *The Complete Works of Stephen Charnock, B.D.*, 5 vols., Nichol edition, 1864-1866, vol. 1, p. 305.
[22] Burroughs, *op. cit.*, pp. 181-6.
[23] Wells, *op. cit.*, pp. 315-6.
[24] Burroughs, *op. cit.*, pp. 189-191.
[25] *Cripplegate Exercises*, vol. 2, p. 57.
[26] Swinnock, *op. cit.*, pp. 167-8.
[27] Burroughs, *op. cit.*, pp. 192-3.
[28] Gillespie, *Dispute Against The English Popish Ceremonies*, 1660, p. 123, quoted by Horton Davies, *The Worship of the English Puritans*, Dacre Press, 1948, p. 269.
[29] Quoted from Henry Rogers, *The Life and Character of John Howe, M.A.*, R.T.S., 1863, p. 32.
[30] See *Life and Times of Rev. Philip Henry, M.A.*, Nelson, 1848, p. 261.
[31] Benjamin Brook, *The Lives of the Puritans*, 3 vols, 1813, vol. 3, p. 248.

PART THREE   THE PURITAN IN PRIVATE

[1] Robert Bolton, *Instruction for a Right Comforting Afflicted Consciences*, 1640, p. 135.
[2] *ibid.*, p. 350.
[3] *ibid.*, p. 392, quoting from John Downame, *The Christian Warfare*.
[4] *The Rev. Oliver Heywood, B.A.*, 1630-1702; *His Autobiography, Diaries, Anecdote and Event Books*, 4 vols., Turner edition, 1880-1885, vol. 2, p. 60.
[5] Goodwin, *Works*, vol. 3, p. 237.
[6] Christopher Love, *Grace: The Truth and Growth and Different Degrees Thereof*, 1657, pp. 82-3.
[7] Joseph Symonds, *The Case and Cure of a Deserted Soul. Or, a Treatise Concerning the Nature, Kinds, Degrees, Symptoms, Causes, Cure of and Mistakes about Spiritual Desertions*, 1641, pp. 4-7.
[8] Manton, *Works*, vol. 6, p. 81.
[9] *ibid.*, pp. 77-80.
[10] Goodwin, *op. cit.*, p. 239.
[11] Wells, *op. cit.*, pp. 199-200.
[12] Sibbes, *Works*, vol. 2, p. 112.
[13] William Bridge, *A Lifting up for the Downcast*, Banner of Truth reprint, 1961, p. 30.
[14] Goodwin, *op. cit.*, p. 242.
[15] Bridge, *op. cit.*, p. 30.
[16] Goodwin, *op. cit.*, p. 241.
[17] *ibid.*, p. 242.
[18] Bridge, *op. cit.*, p. 31.
[19] Goodwin, *op. cit.*, pp. 244-5.

20 Bridge, *op. cit.*, p. 31.
21 *Letters of Samuel Rutherford*, Ed. A. Bonar, 4th edition, p. 675, (Letter 342).
22 Samuel Rutherford, *The Trial and Triumph of Faith*, 1826 edition, p. 103.
23 Goodwin, *op. cit.*, pp. 288-9.
24 Symonds, *op. cit.*, p. 353.
25 *ibid.*, p. 187.
26 *ibid.*, p. 188.
27 Robert Asty, *Rejoicing in the Lord Jesus in all Cases and Conditions*, Puritan Library reprint, no date, p. 73 (ch. 2, proposition 6).
28 Symonds, *op. cit.*, pp. 197-8.
29 Goodwin, *op. cit.*, p. 302.
30 Bridge, *op. cit.*, pp. 32-3.
31 Goodwin, *op. cit.*, p. 303, c.f. Bolton, *op. cit.*, pp. 509-510.
32 Manton, *Works*, vol. 6, p. 81.
33 *The Complete Works of Thomas Brooks*, 6 vols, 1866-1867, Nichol edition, vol. 1, p. 378.
34 Goodwin, *op. cit.*, pp. 304-5.
35 Matthew Lawrence, *The Use and Practice of Faith*, 1657, p. 29.
36 *ibid.*, p. 30.
37 Flavel, *Works*, vol. 1, p. 417.
38 Symonds, *op. cit.*, p. 145.
39 See *ad loc.*
40 Symonds, *op. cit.*, p. 514.
41 Bridge, *op. cit.*, p. 32.
42 Goodwin, *op. cit.*, p. 306.
43 Bolton, *op. cit.*, p. 510.
44 Symonds, *op. cit.*, p. 520.
45 *ibid.*, pp. 519-520.
46 Goodwin, *op. cit.*, p. 306.
47 Symonds, *op. cit.*, p. 353.
48 *ibid.*, p. 353.
49 *ibid.*, p. 522.
50 Christopher Love, *The Dejected Soul's Cure*, 1657 p. 62 (Numbered wrongly as p. 52).
51 Goodwin, *op. cit.*, p. 306.
52 Love, *op. cit.*, p. 7, c.f. Symonds, *op. cit.*, p. 353.
53 Rutherford, *Letters*, p. 446 (Letter 234).
54 Bolton, *op. cit.*, p. 516.
55 Symonds, *op. cit.*, pp. 533-4.
56 *ibid.*, p. 357.
57 *ibid.*, p. 355.
58 Love, *Grace: The Truth and Growth*, 1657, p. 88.
59 Love, *The Dejected Soul's Cure*, 1657, pp. 58-9.
60 *ibid.*, p. 60.
61 Symonds, *op. cit.*, pp. 152-3.
62 *ibid.*, p. 523.
63 Love, *op. cit*, p. 57.
64 *ibid.*, p. 58.
65 Love, *Grace: The Truth and Growth*, p. 88.
66 Obadiah Sedgwick, *The Anatomy of Secret Sins* . . ., 1660, p. 121.
67 Joseph Caryl, *An Exposition with Practical Observations upon the Book of Job*, 2 folio vols., 1676, vol. 1, p. 1306.
68 *ibid.*, p. 1307.
69 Bolton, *op. cit.*, p. 507.
70 *ibid.*, p. 508.
71 Caryl, *op. cit.*, p. 1307.
72 Nehemiah Rogers, *The True Convert* 1632, part 3, p. 51.
73 Goodwin, *op. cit.*, p. 293.
74 *ibid.*
75 Bridge, *op. cit.*, pp. 35-6.
76 Owen, *Works*, *op. cit.*, vol. 2, p. 265.
77 Sibbes, *Works*, *op. cit.*, vol. 5, p. 415.
78 *ibid.*, p. 414.

[79] Owen, *op. cit.*, p. 265.
[80] John Owen, *An Exposition of Hebrews*, see *ad loc.*, Heb. 3:7-11, Obs. 25.
[81] Sibbes, *op. cit.*, p. 415.
[82] Symonds, *op. cit.*, p. 167.
[83] Love, *Grace: The Truth and Growth*, *op. cit.*, p. 87.
[84] Lawrence, *op. cit.*, p. 275.
[85] Brooks, *op. cit.*, p. 375.
[86] Symonds, *op. cit.*, pp. 516-7.
[87] Bolton, *op. cit.*, p. 518.
[88] Bridge, *op. cit.*, p. 33.
[89] *ibid.*, p. 33.
[90] Goodwin, *op. cit.*, p. 289.
[91] *ibid.*
[92] Nathaniel Whiting, *Old Jacob's Altar Newly Repaired*, 1659, pp. 200-2.
[93] Love, *Dejected Soul's Cure*, p. 66.
[94] Goodwin, *op. cit.*, p. 249.
[95] Love, *Grace: The Truth and Growth*, p. 86.
[96] Brooks, *Works*, vol. 3, p. 296.
[97] Brooks, *Works*, vol. 4, p. 260.
[98] *Cripplegate Exercises*, vol. 3, p. 255-6.
[99] *ibid.*, p. 256.
[100] *ibid.*, pp. 280-283.
[101] Brooks, *op. cit.*, p. 260.
[102] Goodwin, *op. cit.*, p. 250.
[103] *ibid.*, p. 252.
[104] *ibid.*, pp. 253-4.
[105] *ibid.*, p. 256.
[106] *ibid.*, p. 260.
[107] Sibbes, *Works*, vol. 1, p. 142.
[108] *ibid.*, p. 134.
[109] *ibid.*, p. 134.
[110] Love, *op. cit.*, p. 89.
[111] Love, *The Dejected Soul's Cure*, *op. cit.*, pp. 64-5.
[112] Richard Gilpin, *Demonologia Sacra: or A Treatise of Satan's Temptations*, reprint, Edinburgh, 1735, p. 284.
[113] *ibid.*, p. 284.
[114] *ibid.*, pp. 286-7.
[115] *ibid.*, pp. 287-8.
[116] Goodwin, *op. cit.*, p. 262.
[117] *ibid.*, p. 263.
[118] Gilpin, *op. cit.*, pp. 360-2.
[119] *ibid.*, p. 362.
[120] *ibid.*, p. 361.
[121] *ibid.*, p. 362.
[122] *ibid.*, p. 363.
[123] *ibid.*, pp. 367-8.
[124] *ibid.*, p. 372.
[125] *ibid.*, p. 373.
[126] *ibid.*, p. 374.
[127] *ibid.*, p. 375.
[128] Thomas Harrison, *Topica Sacra or Spiritual Logick*, reprint, Aberdeen, 1770, p. 55.
[129] *ibid.*, p. 56.
[130] *ibid.*, p. 85.
[131] *ibid.*, p. 86.
[132] *ibid.*, p. 86.
[133] *ibid.*, p. 87.
[134] Gilpin, *op. cit.*, p. 379.
[135] *ibid.*, pp. 379-380.
[136] *ibid.*, p. 381.
[137] *ibid.*, pp. 382-384.
[138] *ibid.*, p. 385.
[139] *ibid.*, p. 386.

[140] In *Spiritual Opticks* by Nathaniel Culverwell, 1668, *The White Stone: or a Learned and Choice Treatise of Assurance*, p. 111.
[141] *ibid.*, p. 115.
[142] Symonds, *op. cit.*, p. 226.
[143] Goodwin, *op. cit.*, p. 269.
[144] William Spurstowe, *The Wiles of Satan*, p. 83, in *The Spiritual Chemist*, 1666.
[145] Goodwin, *op. cit.*, p. 269.
[146] Love, *Grace: The Truth and Growth*, p. 43.
[147] *Cripplegate Exercises*, vol. 1, p. 21.
[148] *ibid.*
[149] Simon Ford, *The Spirit of Bondage and Adoption*, 1655, p. 285.
[150] Goodwin, *op. cit.*, pp. 279-283.
[151] Gilpin, *op. cit.*, p. 389.
[152] *ibid.*
[153] *ibid.*, pp. 422-3.
[154] *ibid.*, pp. 355-7.
[155] *ibid.*, pp. 357-8.
[156] *ibid.*, p. 359.
[157] Symonds, *op. cit.*, pp. 12 and 15.
[158] *ibid.*, p. 240.
[159] Lawrence, *op. cit.*, pp. 273-4.
[160] *ibid.*, p. 50.
[161] Love, *The Dejected Soul's Cure*, pp. 68-75.
[162] Bridge, *op. cit.*, p. 187.
[163] Bolton, *op. cit.*, pp. 134-303.
[164] *ibid.*, p. 194.
[165] Caryl, *op. cit.*, p. 700.
[166] Sibbes, *Works*, vol. 1, p. 197, in *The Soul's Conflict and Victory over itself by Faith*.
[167] *ibid.*, p. 198.
[168] *ibid.*
[169] Symonds, *op. cit.*, p. 551.
[170] *ibid.*, pp. 551-2.
[171] Goodwin, *op. cit.*, pp. 332 and 336.
[172] Manton, *Works*, vol. 6, p. 81.
[173] Goodwin, *op. cit.*, p. 324.
[174] Sibbes, *Works*, vol. 7, p. 59.
[175] *ibid.*, vol. 1, p. 203.
[176] Goodwin, *op. cit.*, p. 325.
[177] Jeremiah Burroughs, *Treatise on Matt.* 11:28, *Christ Inviting Sinners to Come to Him for Rest*, 1659, pp. 372-8.
[178] *ibid.*, p. 378.
[179] Thomas Sharp, M.A., *Divine Comforts Antidoting Inward Perplexities of Mind* (Posthumously published 1700), p. 266.
[180] Sibbes, *Works*, vol. 1, p. 207.
[181] *ibid.*
[182] *ibid.*, p. 208.
[183] *Cripplegate Exercises*, vol. 1, p. 396.
[184] Sibbes, *op. cit.*, p. 212.
[185] Goodwin, *op. cit.*, p. 319.
[186] *ibid.*, p. 320.
[187] William Spurstowe, D.D., *The Wells of Salvation Opened: or A Treatise . . . of Gospel Promises and Rules for a Right Application of Them*, 1654.
[188] *ibid.*, p. 30.
[189] *ibid.*, p. 29.
[190] *ibid.*, p. 30.
[191] *ibid.*, pp. 39-40.
[192] *ibid.*, p. 40.
[193] *ibid.*, pp. 44-45.
[194] *ibid.*, p. 48.
[195] *ibid.*, p. 50.
[196] Bridge, *op. cit.*, p. 44.
[197] Spurstowe, *op. cit.*, pp. 47-48.
[198] *ibid.*, p. 47.

[199] *ibid.*, p. 66.
[200] *ibid.*, p. 71.
[201] *ibid.*, p. 77.
[202] *ibid.*, pp. 78-9.
[203] *ibid.*, pp. 83-4.
[204] *ibid.*, 84-5.
[205] *ibid.*, p. 90.
[206] *ibid.*, pp. 106-7.
[207] *ibid.*, p. 108.
[208] *ibid.*, pp. 255-6.
[209] Goodwin, *op. cit.*, p. 321.
[210] Sharp, *op. cit.*, p. 140.
[211] *ibid.*, pp. 141-2.
[212] Sibbes, *op. cit.*, p. 220.
[213] *ibid.*
[214] Goodwin, *op. cit.*, p. 325.
[215] *Cripplegate Exercises*, vol. 4, p. 80.
[216] *ibid.*, pp. 102-6.
[217] *ibid.*, pp. 106-7.
[218] *ibid.*, pp. 107-9.
[219] *ibid.*, pp. 109-110.
[220] Bridge, *op. cit.*, p. 68.
[221] Love, *op. cit.*, pp. 17-19.
[222] *ibid.*, pp. 19-20.
[223] *ibid.*, p. 194.
[224] *ibid.*, pp. 192-4 (faulty pagination), also pp. 18-21.
[225] *ibid.*, pp. 20-2.
[226] *ibid.*, p. 22.
[227] *ibid.*, pp. 22-3.
[228] *ibid.*, p. 195.
[229] *ibid.*, pp. 181-3.
[230] *ibid.*, pp. 202-7.
[231] *ibid.*, pp. 211-2.
[232] *ibid.*, pp. 36-8.
[233] Owen, *Works, op. cit.*, vol. 6, p. 549.
[234] Sibbes, *op. cit.*, p. 249.
[235] *ibid.*, p. 252.
[236] Love, *op. cit.*, p. 60.
[237] Asty, *op. cit.*, p. 89 (ch. IV).
[238] *ibid.*, pp. 93-94 (ch. IV, Direction VII).
[239] Rutherford, *Trial and Triumph of Faith*, p. 105.
[240] Goodwin, *op. cit.*, p. 320 (Goodwin here mistakenly writes 'David' for 'Asaph').
[241] *ibid.*, p. 321.
[242] *ibid.*, p. 322.
[243] Asty, *op. cit.*, p. 94 (ch. IV, Direction VIII).
[244] Goodwin, *op. cit.*, pp. 322-3.
[245] *ibid.*, p. 323.
[246] *ibid.*
[247] Bridge, *op. cit.*, p. 42.
[248] *ibid.*, p. 43.
[249] Symonds, *op. cit.*, pp. 375-9, 380.
[250] Goodwin, *op. cit.*, p. 330.
[251] *ibid.*, pp. 330-1.
[252] *ibid.*, p. 331.
[253] *ibid.*, p. 331.
[254] Asty, *op. cit.*, p. 92 (ch. IV, Direction V).
[255] Jeremiah Burroughs, *Two Treatises . . . of Earthly Mindedness . . . of Conversing in Heaven, and Walking with God*, 1656, p. 338.
[256] *ibid.*, p. 337.
[257] Symonds, *op. cit.*, p. 380.
[258] *ibid.*, 380-2.
[259] Sibbes, *op. cit.*, p. 149.

BIBLIOGRAPHY OF PRIMARY WORKS QUOTED

Samuel Annesley	'How we may give Christ a Satisfying Account, why we attend upon the Ministry of the Word,' *The Morning Exercises at Cripplegate* . . ., vol. 4.
	'How we may be universally and exactly conscientious,' *The Morning Exercises at Cripplegate* . . ., vol. 1.
Robert Asty	*Rejoicing in the Lord Jesus in all Cases and Conditions.*
William Attersol	*A Commentary upon the Epistle of Saint Paul to Philemon,* folio (1633).
Richard Baxter	*Gildas Silvianus: The Reformed Pastor,* 2nd edition (1657).
	'The Cure of Melancholy and Overmuch Sorrow,' *The Morning Exercises at Cripplegate* . . ., vol. 3.
Paul Bayne	*A Commentary upon Ephesians,* folio (1658).
Robert Bolton	*Instruction for a Right Comforting Afflicted Consciences* (1640).
William Bridge	*A Lifting up for the Downcast* (1648), (Banner of Truth Reprint, 1961).
Thomas Brooks	'The Mute Christian under the Smarting Rod' (1659), *Works,* Nichol edition, vol. 1.
	'A Cabinet of Jewels' (1669), *Works,* vol. 3.
	'The Crown and Glory of Christianity' (1662), *Works,* vol. 4.
Jeremiah Burroughs	*Gospel Worship* (1648).
	Christ Inviting Sinners to Come to Him for Rest (1659).
	Two Treatises . . . of Earthly Mindedness . . . of Conversing in Heaven and Walking with God (1656).
Nicholas Byfield	*An Exposition upon the Epistle to the Colossians,* folio (1649).
Joseph Caryl	*An Exposition with Practical Observations Upon the Book of Job,* 12 vols. quarto, or 2 vols. folio (1676).
Stephen Charnock	'Discourses on the Existence and Attributes of God (1681-2), *Works,* Nichol edition, vol. 1.
Nathaniel Culverwell	'The White Stone: or a Learned and Choice Treatise of Assurance,' *Spiritual Opticks* (1668).
John Downame	*The Christian Warfare,* 4th edition (1634).
James Durham	*A Commentary upon The Book of the Revelation,* quarto (1680).
John Flavel	'The Character of a Complete Evangelical Pastor,' *Works* (Banner of Truth Reprint, 1968), vol. 5.
	'The Fountain of Life Opened Up,' *Works,* vol. 1.
Simon Ford	*The Spirit of Bondage and Adoption* (1655).
Richard Gilpin	*Demonologia Sacra: or A Treatise of Satan's Temptations* (1677), quoted as reprint (1735).
Thomas Goodwin	'The Constitution, Right Order and Government of Churches of Christ,' *Works,* Nichol edition, vol. 11.
	'A Child of Light Walking in Darkness,' *Works,* Nichol edition, vol. 3.
Thomas Hall	*A Practical and Polemical Commentary . . . upon The Third and Fourth Chapters of the Latter Epistle of St. Paul to Timothy,* folio (1659).
Thomas Harrison	*Topica Sacra or Spiritual Logick* reprint (1770).
Oliver Heywood	*His Autobiography, Diaries, Anecdote and Event Books,* Turner edition, vol. 2.
Arthur Hildersham	*152 Lectures upon Psalm 51,* folio (1642).
Matthew Lawrence	*The Use and Practice of Faith* (1657).
Christopher Love	*Grace: the Truth and Growth and Different Degrees Thereof* (1657).
	The Dejected Soul's Cure (1657).
Thomas Lye	'How are we to live by Faith on Divine Providence?' *The Morning Exercises at Cripplegate* . . ., vol. 1.

Thomas Manton	A Practical Commentary . . . on the Epistle of James,' *Works*, Nisbet edition, vol. 4.
	'Sermons upon the 119th Psalm,' folio (1681), *Works*, vol. 6.
John Mayer	*Praxis Theologica: or the Epistle of the Apostle St. James . . . Resolved* (1629).
John Owen	'An Exposition of the Epistle to the Hebrews' *Works*, Goold edition.
	'Of Communion with God the Father, Son and Holy Ghost each Person Distinctly in Love, Grace and Consolation,' *Works*, Goold edition vol. 2.
	'An Exposition upon Psalm 130,' *Works*, Goold edition, vol. 6.
Elnathan Parr	*Works*, folio (1633).
William Perkins	'Of the Calling of the Ministry,' Two Treatises in *Works* (1618), vol. 3.
Edward Reynolds	'The Preaching of Christ' opened in a sermon (1661), *Works*, vol. 5, ed. Chalmers.
Nehemiah Rogers	*The True Convert* (1632).
Richard Rogers	*Seven Treatises Containing such Directions as are gathered out of the Holie Scriptures leading and guiding to true happiness both in this life and in the life to come . . . in the which . . . Christians may learne how to lead a godly and comfortable life every day* (1603).
Samuel Rutherford	*Letters of Samuel Rutherford*, A. Bonar.
	The Trial and Triumph of Faith.
Obadiah Sedgwick	The Anatomy of Sins . . . (1660).
Thomas Sharp	*Divine Comforts Antidoting Inward Perplexities of Mind* (1700).
Richard Sibbes	'The Fountain Opened' (1638), *Works* Grosart edition, vol. 5.
	'Bowels Opened' (1639), *Works*, vol. 2.
	'The Soul's Conflict and Victory over itself by Faith' (1635), *Works*, vol. 1.
	'Discouragement's Recovery' (1629), *Works*, vol. 7.
Henry Smith	'The Trial of True Spirits,' *Works*, Nichol edition, vol. 2.
William Spurstowe	'The Wiles of Satan,' *The Spiritual Chemist* (1666).
	The Wells of Salvation Opened: or A Treatise . . . of Gospel Promises and Rules for a Right Application of Them (1654).
George Swinnock	'The Christian Man's Calling' (part one), *Works*, Nichol edition, vol. 1.
Matthew Sylvester	'How may a Gracious Person from whom God hides his face Trust in the Lord as his God?' *The Morning Exercises at Cripplegate . . .*, vol. 4.
Joseph Symonds	*The Case and Cure of a Deserted Soul or a Treatise Concerning the Nature, Kinds, Degrees, Symptoms, Causes, Cure of and Mistakes about Spiritual Desertions* (1641).
Robert Traill	'A Sermon on By What Means May Ministers Best Win Souls' (1682).
John Wells	*The Practical Sabbatarian: or Sabbath Holiness Crowned with Superlative Happiness* (1668).
Thomas White	'Of Effectual Calling,' *The Morning Exercises at Cripplegate, St. Giles in the Fields and in Southwark*, Nichol edition, vol. 5.
Nathaniel Whiting	*Old Jacob's Altar Newly Repaired* (1659).

PUBLISHED BOOKS FROM
THE BIBLIOGRAPHY

Soli Deo Gloria Publications
P.O. Box 451, Morgan, PA 15064

Richard Baxter. *The Reformed Pastor*
(Volume 4 of *The Practical Works of Richard Baxter*), 1990.

Robert Bolton. *A Treatise on Comforting Afflicted Consciences*,
1991.

William Bridge. "A Lifting Up for the Downcast," in
volume 2 of *The Works of William Bridge* (5 volumes), 1989.

Benjamin Brooks. *Lives of the Puritans* (3 volumes), 1994.

Jeremiah Burroughs. *Gospel Worship*, 1990.
A Treatise on Earthly-Mindedness, 1991.

Joseph Caryl. *Bible Thoughts* (ed. by Ingram Cobbin, excerpts
from *An Exposition with Practical Observations Upon the Book of
Job*), 1995

Christopher Love. *Grace: the Truth and Growth and Different
Degrees Thereof*, 1997

Obadiah Sedgwick. *Anatomy of Secret Sins*, 1995.

Joseph Symonds. *The Case and Cure of a Deserted Soul*, 1996

The Banner of Truth Trust
P.O. Box 621, Carlisle, PA 17013

The Works of Thomas Brooks (6 volumes), 1980.

The Works of John Flavel (6 volumes), 1968.

The Works of John Owen (16 volumes), 1968.

John Owen. *A Commentary on Hebrews* (7 volumes), 1996

Samuel Rutherford. *Letters of Samuel Rutherford,* 1985.

The Works of Richard Sibbes (7 volumes), 1982.

The Works of George Swinnock (5 volumes), 1992.

Select Practical Writings of Robert Trail (2 volumes), 1975.

Old Paths Publications
223 Princeton Road, Audubon, NJ 08106

James Fraser. *Treatise on Sanctification,* 1992.

Richard Owen Roberts
P.O. Box 21, Wheaton, IL 60189

Puritan Sermons (1659–1689): The Morning Exercises at Cripplegate (6 volumes), 1981.

Tanski Publications
P.O. Box 6673, Eureka CA 95502

The Works of Thomas Goodwin (12 volumes), 1997.